Condition Noted

KITCHENER PUBLIC LIBRARY
3 9098 01490
Y0-AWV-984

06/04

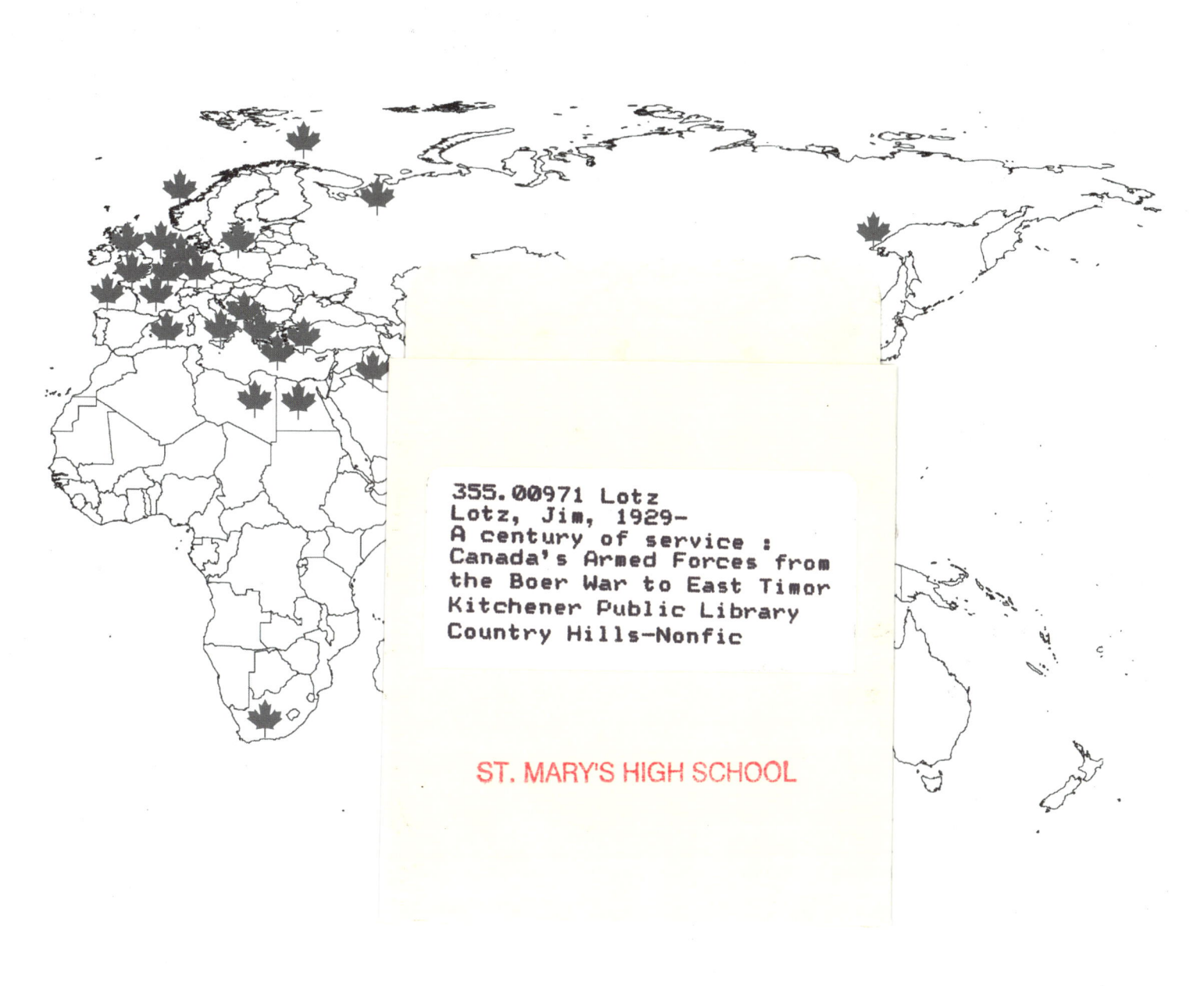

355.00971 Lotz
Lotz, Jim, 1929-
A century of service :
Canada's Armed Forces from
the Boer War to East Timor
Kitchener Public Library
Country Hills-Nonfic

ST. MARY'S HIGH SCHOOL

A CENTURY OF SERVICE

*Canada's Armed Forces
from the Boer War to East Timor*

Jim Lotz

Consulting Editor: Col (Ret'd) John Boileau

Foreword by Her Excellency
the Rt. Honourable Adrienne Clarkson, Governor General of Canada
and Commander–in–Chief, Canadian Forces

The Nova Scotia International Tattoo Society 2000

Copyright 2000 Jim Lotz

All rights reserved. No part of this work may be reproduced or used in any form or by any means, electronic or mechanical, including photocopying, recording or any information storage or retrieval system without the prior written permission of the publisher.

Design: Ken Webb Design
Printed and bound in Canada by Print Atlantic, Dartmouth

Main entry under title:

    A Century of Service

    ISBN 0-9687710-0-9

The Nova Scotia International Tattoo Society,
1586 Queen Street
Halifax, NS, B3J 2J1
Canada

Publication Date: November 11, 2000

This book is dedicated to all Canadian service men and women — past, present and future.

With gratitude and admiration.

CONTENTS

Acknowledgements	1
Foreword by Her Excellency the Rt. Honourable Adrienne Clarkson	3
Preface by VAdm (Ret'd) Lynn Mason	3
Introduction	4
The Boer War, 1899-1902	8
The First World War, 1914-1918	
On Land	14
In The Air	40
At Sea	49
Canada's First Nations Go to War	52
The Mounties' Military Tradition	54
The Second World War, 1939-1945	
On Land	58
Hong Kong, December, 1941	
Dieppe, August 19, 1942	
Sicily and Italy, 1943-45	
D-Day to V-E Day, June 6, 1944 – May 7, 1945	
In the Air	97
At Sea	121
Canada's Merchant Navy at War	137
The End of the War	142
The Korean Conflict, 1950-1953	145
Canada in NATO and NORAD: The Cold War and Some Hot Ones	151
Citizens in Service: The Reserves	156
The Peaceful Uses of Canada's Armed Forces.	157
Further Reading	179
The Author and the Consulting Editor	181

ACKNOWLEDGEMENTS

Each year, The Nova Scotia International Tattoo pays tribute to an aspect of Canada's military history. This book continues and expands this tradition. Ian Fraser, Producer/Director of the Tattoo supported the idea of a book that would put a human face on Canada's distinguished record in war and peacekeeping. I am grateful to Ian for this opportunity to tell these stories. I am also appreciative of the help and support of the members of his staff – Ann Montague, Barbara MacLeod, Iona Allen, and especially Katherine MacDougall who looked after numerous details as the book moved towards publication.

John Boileau was everything an editor should be – and more. His encyclopedic knowledge, attention to detail, respect for language and fine eye for illustrations for the text proved invaluable at every stage of the book. I could not have written this book without his help and enthusiastic presence. However, I alone am responsible for any errors, omissions, or misinterpretations in it. As always, my wife Pat provided an invaluable sounding board and final copy editor. Ken Webb, the designer, and Calvin Ripley and his team at Print Atlantic brought their skills to bear on this undertaking.

Many others helped to take this book from an idea to a finished product. They include Lorraine Gailey of Veterans' Affairs Canada; Henry Bishop, the Black Cultural Centre; Dr. Peter Liddle, The Second World War Experience Centre, Leeds, England; Cpl. Annette Lotz and Sgt. Mary Nangle,CD; M/Cpl Heather Bruce; Major (Ret'd) Bill Pell.

I would also like to acknowledge the following for their specific contributions to the book.

BGen Greg Mitchell, CD, Commander Land Force Atlantic Area and Chairman of the Army Museum, Halifax Citadel (permission to use photos from Army Museum and LFAAHQ Graphic Artist to draw maps)

Col (Ret'd) Bruce Gilchrist, CD, Vice Chairman of the Army Museum, Halifax Citadel (arrangements to use photos from Army Museum and LFAAHQ Graphic Artist)

Rod MacLean, Curator of the Army Museum, Halifax Citadel (assistance in selecting photos from Army Museum)

WO (Ret'd) Don LaPointe, CD, Graphic Artist Land Force Atlantic Area Headquarters (drawing of all maps)

Marilyn Gurney, Director of the Maritime Command Museum (permission to use and assistance in selecting photos from Maritime Command Museum)

LCol (Ret'd) Chuck Coffen, CD, Curator of the Shearwater Aviation Museum (permission to use photos from the Shearwater Aviation Museum)

Christine Duffy, Librarian/ Archivist of the Shearwater Aviation Museum (assistance in selecting photos from the Shearwater Aviation Museum)

AnhThu Lauzon, Acting Director of Intellectual Property National Defence Headquarters (permission to use DND photos)

Tracey Biron, Brian O'Donnell, Shauna MacLeod (retyping of manuscript)

Deidre Jackson, Office of the Governor General And the splendid people at the National Archives and the National Library of Canada for prompt and efficient service.

Every attempt has been made to identify the owners of the illustrations. We regret any errors or omissions.

Photo Credits:
AMHC: Army Museum Halifax Citadel
DND: Department of National Defence
JBB: John Boileau
LDSH: Lord Strathcona's Horse
MCM: Maritime Command Museum
NAC: National Archives of Canada
RCMI: Royal Canadian Military Institute
SAM: Shearwater Aviation Museum

This project generously supported by:

unisource   Print Atlantic

FOREWORD

RIDEAU HALL

Canada's history of military achievement rings with names that contain worlds of meaning and emotion - Ypres, Vimy Ridge, Dieppe, the beaches of Normandy, and Korea. In these places, there were acts of bravery and heroism that are etched into our collective memory. These places are milestones in the Canadian journey, where soldiers stood in defence of our values and earned our thanks and admiration.

Those battlefields, thousands of kilometres from our shores, helped define who we are, what we believe in and on what principles we stand and will not yield. Yet they also exacted a great loss - the lives and potential of thousands of Canadians.

We will never know what those who died in cold trenches, mine-strewn fields, sunken ships or shattered planes might have contributed to our society. But their sacrifices taught us that we should never accept the unbearable heartbreak of war, but work with every effort for peace. Proudly, we have become the very definition of peacekeeping for the international community, and today our military personnel devote much of their time to preventing war.

Behind these watershed events are the faces, names and stories of men and women-too often, much too young-who put themselves on the front lines, who took on dangerous and horrifying duties when their country called. Many of them never came home, others returned to their families bearing mental or physical scars. All of them served their country so that we can live in a prosperous, compassionate and free society.

We owe a tremendous debt to all of them, a debt that we can never properly repay. We can, however, honour and cherish their stories. We must ensure that long-ago accomplishments are not diminished by time and that those women and men are never lost from our hearts.

A Century of Service: Canada's Armed Forces From the Boer War to East Timor is a fitting tribute to the achievements, professionalism and commitment of the Canadian Armed Forces. It is an eloquent expression of gratitude to the generations of Canadian soldiers who have served selflessly and with honour so that our country's dreams could flourish.

As Commander-in-Chief of the Canadian Forces, I congratulate the Nova Scotia International Tattoo Society for publishing *A Century of Service,* and I particularly thank Jim Lotz and Colonel John B. Boileau. I hope it reminds us that the ideals that so many young Canadians fought to preserve - democracy, peace, freedom and tolerance - are still moral lights that guide us today.

Adrienne Clarkson

PREFACE

For many years Jim Lotz has written articles that deal with the contribution of Canada's armed forces in the development of our country for the annual souvenir program of The Nova Scotia International Tattoo.

These short items were unique not just because they were immensely readable and paid tribute to Canada's military traditions, but because they put a very human face on the Canadian Forces. They focused on the significant military events that helped shape our nation and on the young Canadian men and women who served in our armed forces in peace, in war, and in that gray area of peacekeeping that lies somewhere between.

When we were searching for a millennium project, it became obvious to us that the perfect project was, to some degree, already underway. Why not ask Jim to expand those short articles that have appeared in our programs every year, add to them and give us his version of what the people serving in Canada's Navy, Army and Air Force have accomplished over the past century – from the Boer War in 1900 to East Timor a hundred years later?

In *A Century of Service*, he has done just that.

What he has given us is not the cold stuff of military history tomes, nor is it a ponderous examination of the exploits of general and flag officers. It is the story of the achievements of ordinary Canadians in war, in peace and in peacekeeping - that enormously frustrating and vital role that Canadians have performed so well for nearly five decades. These are real stories about real people and are far more dramatic than any fictional accounts.

If there is a dominant theme in this book, it is the ability of Canadians in times of conflict to show great initiative and courage within the framework of sound military discipline - a fact that has been praised more by others than by Canadians. Jim Lotz has also recognized that maintaining the discipline and initiative that has served the Canadian Forces so well in the past, is the most significant challenge facing our military in the third millennium.

But there is another element in this book that comes through clearly both in the words and insights of the young Canadians who served and in the accounts of their achievements. That element is the characteristic modesty that has been so typical when those who have served Canada have been asked to tell their stories. It is a characteristic that has helped to make this great nation what it is today.

Every Canadian should read this book.

They will be far richer for the experience and they will come away not only with a sense of pride but also with a sense of discovery that ordinary Canadians can do extraordinary things.

VAdm (Ret'd) Lynn Mason,
Chairman,
The Nova Scotia International
Tattoo Society

INTRODUCTION

*"Lay them with all that is most living,
In light transcendent, In the ageless aisles of silence,
with the Immortals that saved the world".*

Lines written in red upon the Book of Remembrance,
Memorial Chamber, Parliament Buildings, Ottawa.

On May 28 this year, a moving ceremony took place in Ottawa. After lying in state in the Parliament Buildings, Canada's Unknown Soldier was interred at the National War Memorial in Confederation Square. This man died in the assault on Vimy Ridge in France in April 1917. Fighting together for the first time, four Canadian divisions took a German position that had been deemed impregnable. This victory came at heavy cost – 3,598 dead and 7,004 wounded. Those who took part in the battle and historians recognized the event as marking a new sense of nationhood in Canada.

The Unknown Soldier serves as a symbol and a national presence for 112,000 Canadian men and women lost in the wars of the 20th Century. Their remains lie in 75 countries around the world: 27,000 of the lost dead have no known graves. At the internment ceremony, spontaneous applause broke out as a column of veterans marched into Confederation Square.

A few of those who served in the First World War are still with us, but the average age of Second World War veterans is 78, that of those who survived the Korean War, 70. I've spoken to a number of these men, and they all have one thing in common. They are modest about their time in Canada's Armed Forces. None see themselves as heroes, but talk simply about "doing a job". All remember comrades who did not survive and the sadness has stayed with them all their days. But many recall the good times, the comradeship, the sense of purpose, the ways they outwitted the enemy – and their own commanders. From their reminiscences emerges the unique Canadian military style, combining discipline and boldness. There has never been a war for a Canadian cause. But when called to serve, the members of Canada's services gained a reputation as fierce fighters who showed tenacity and courage when handed the toughest assignments. Yet their achievements are little recognized and honoured in Canada.

In 1993, I travelled back in time to the battlefields of the Western Front. With a British tour group, I visited many of the places where Canada's soldiers served, suffered and died during the First World War. I gained a new perspective on how others view this country's contribution to the Allied victory. Many of the people on the tour expressed appreciation for Canada's efforts. "It was not your war," one of them said. Someone asked me if Canadians felt any resentment about what the war cost their country. I told her that I'd never heard any expressions of regret, rather, it seems, many Canadians simply don't know – or care – about our nation's splendid record in war.

More and more Canadians are visiting the places where their fellow countrymen served, and all return home changed after seeing the sacrifices that they made. Most of the countryside in Northern France and Flanders consists of flat land with low ridges rising from it. Thousands of men died attacking and defending them. The land, green and fruitful now, yields "iron harvests" through the year – shells, bullets, rusted rifles. And from time to time, badges, buttons and scraps of clothing emerge from the soil. Pvt. David Carlson, a 19 year old farm boy from Alberta vanished in the fog of war in September 1916, during the Canadian attack on Courcelette. In 1999, a tourist found the remains of this member of the 8th Battalion of the Canadian Expeditionary Force. The young man who left Canada in search of adventure and from a sense of duty, now lies with comrades in the military cemetery at Pozières, one of the hundreds of silent cities that dot the land. Designed to resemble English country gardens and beautifully maintained by the Commonwealth War Graves Commission, their rows and rows of white headstones convey an almost unbearable sense of loss, lives cut short after they had barely begun.

Some of the headstones carry epitaphs. Lt. J.H. Stewart of the Princess Patricia's died on June 17, 1915, aged 23:

> "He Lived Cleanly
> And Had Died Nobly
> Even as he would have wished
> Strong to the Last".

At Thiepval, the Menin Gate in Ypres, Tyne Cot and atop Vimy Ridge are recorded the names of those whose bodies were never found. The names go on and on and on … An Englishwoman on the tour said "You'll be shattered by Vimy". The Canadian front line lay very close to that of the Germans at the foot of the ridge. It does not take long to walk to the summit of the ridge. Sheep now safely graze here, but the battlefield remains a deadly place. Barbed wire encloses areas marked "Danger. No Entry. Undetected Explosives". On the summit stands the magnificent monument commemorating the Canadian victory of April 1917, and those who died in the attack. The architect claimed that a dream inspired its design. Twin pillars rise starkly into the sky, and figures of Peace, Truth, Justice and Knowledge mourn at its base. The names of 11,000 of the lost dead are inscribed on the monument. They were being lost again through erosion until the Federal government became aware of the problem and began to look for ways of preserving this symbol of Canadian sacrifice. In the memorial book at a cemetery at the base of the ridge, an entry says simply: "Thank You, Canada".

I returned from my tour of the Western Front very proud of being a Canadian – and very aware of the gratitude that others had shown for the contributions made by members of our armed forces in the First World War. In cemeteries in the Netherlands and elsewhere lie the bodies of those who died in the Second World War, their graves mute witnesses to the cost of that conflict. In recent years, as our veterans age, more and more young Canadians have become aware of the extraordinary contribution that this country has made in war and peacekeeping. More and more people are attending ceremonies on Remembrance Day in silent tribute to those who served.

This book seeks to keep the memory of the Canadian men and women of our Armed Forces green. As much as possible, it tells the story of their deeds in peace and war in their own words. The range of Canadian activities in wartime and peacekeeping is astonishing and little known. Lacking the militaristic traditions of European powers, Canadians had to learn about the fighting on the job. Our service people pioneered peacekeeping in the uneasy years after the end of the Korean War in 1953. In distant lands, they forged a distinct Canadian style of handling the tensions they found. In our troubled and divisive times, we can learn much from what they achieved as we strive to create a stronger and more cohesive nation. No one who has survived war romanticizes or glorifies it, but under extreme conditions, Canadians behaved with courage, tenacity and creativity. These qualities are as vital in peace as they are in war. *A Century of Service* tells only a few of the stories of the men and women who served their country so well and in whose debt we will always remain. In the crucible of war and the perils of peacekeeping, members of Canada's Armed Forces forged a vital part of this nation's identity.

We should recognize and remember their deeds as we look back at the troubled century in which Canada came of age and took her place among the foremost nations of the world.

The BOER WAR
1899 — 1902

"[Our] company was chosen to go and I was lucky enough to get a place and so we were the first Canadians to be under fire."

Pvt. Tom Wallace, C Company,
Royal Canadian Regiment, December 31, 1899, before the attack on Sunnyside Kopje.

Greed for gold and British imperialism sowed the seeds of the South African War. Dutch farmers (Boers) in the Transvaal and Orange Free State bitterly resented the gold seekers who rushed into their republics in search of quick wealth. The Uitlanders (foreigners) demanded rights as citizens and the British government backed them. In October 1899, a Boer army invaded Natal and war began.

Prime Minister Laurier strove valiantly to keep Canada out of the conflict. However, many Canadians found the idea of defending the empire attractive and he was forced to offer troops to Britain to fight in South Africa. The start of the 20th century thus saw the creation of Canada's first expeditionary force, setting a pattern that would be repeated many times.

The first Canadian contingent, commanded by Lt. Col. William Otter, became the 2nd (Special Service) Battalion of the Royal Canadian Regiment (RCR). Its officers and men, most of them untrained, had no idea what awaited them as they disembarked from the troopship *Sardinian* at Cape Town on November 30, 1899. As the Canadians advanced into the Orange Free State, Pvt. Albert Perkins wrote in his diary: "We had a horrible march. The sun was awful. Men fell overcome by heat".

The Canadians distinguished themselves at the Battle of Paardeberg in February 1900. The Boers held off the British for ten days. Then the RCR assaulted their positions. Two companies held their positions as other troops retired after the night attack. When

Members of Strathcona's Horse embark on SS *Monterey* en route to South Africa. DND.

The Dawn of Majuba Day by R.Caton Woodville shows members of the Royal Canadian Regiment rejoicing at the news of the Boer surrender at Paardeberg. RCMI

dawn broke, the Canadians found they overlooked the enemy lines and opened fire. Soon white flags appeared in the Boer trenches.

Realizing the futility of engaging in battle with the British, the Boers formed *kommandos*. Mounted on ponies, hard riding marksmen with Mauser rifles carried out hit and run raids against British positions. To counter them, Canada sent the Royal Canadian Dragoons (RCD), the Canadian Mounted Rifles (CMR) and three batteries of the Royal Canadian Field Artillery (RCFA) to South Africa. Donald Smith, a backer of the Canadian Pacific Railway, put up half a million dollars to equip Strathcona's Horse. Recruited from the North West Mounted Police and western cowboys, the Strathconas began to beat the Boers at their own game. Commanded by "Fighting Sam" Steele, a former Mountie officer, the horsemen served as scouts and flank guards for British columns. One British commander said of them: "I have never served with a nobler, braver or more serviceable body of men." On July 5, 1900, a party of Strathconas encountered twice their number of Boers and retreated under fire. Sgt. Arthur Richardson wheeled his horse around, rescued a wounded comrade and received the first Victoria Cross awarded to a member of a Canadian unit.

In November 1900, the RCD took part in a sharp engagement at Liliefontein. Three

Canadian troops in traditional defensive military pose.

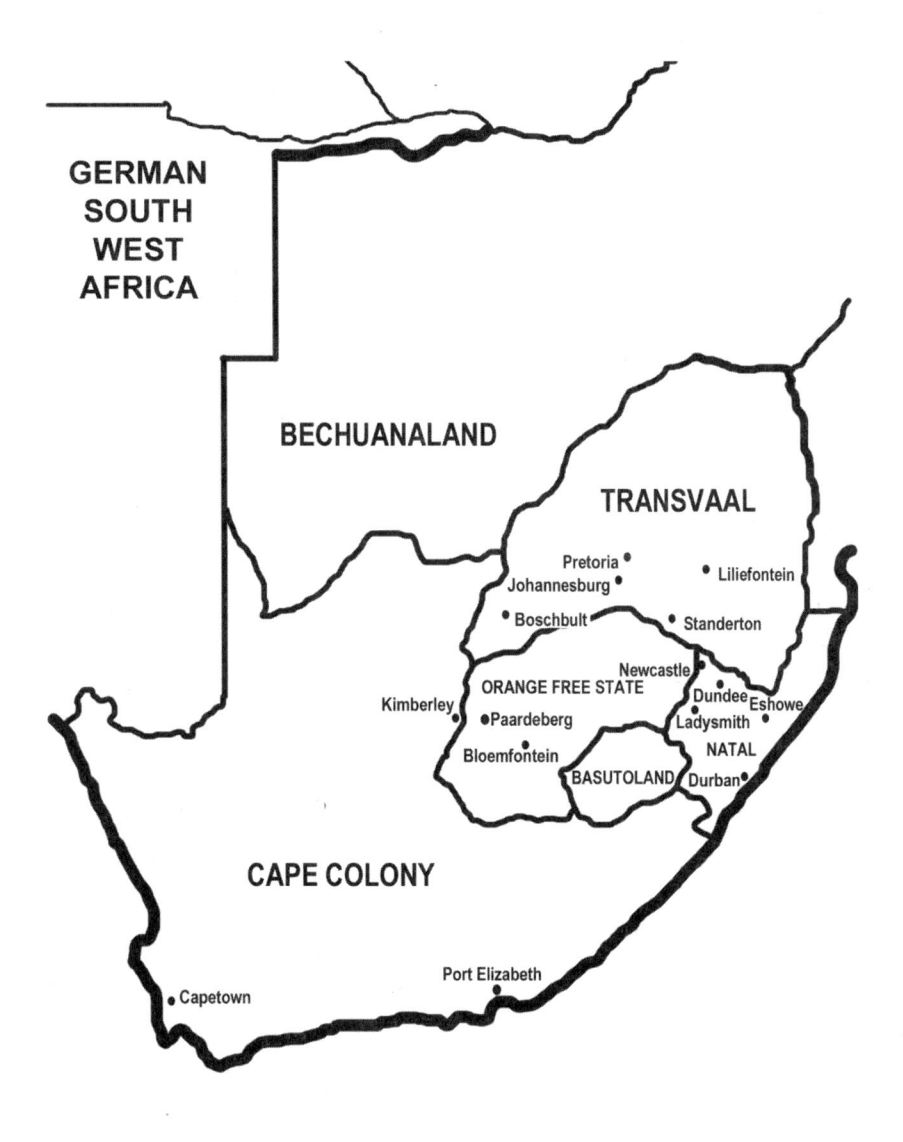

THE BOER WAR
1899-1902

hundred Boers charged, intent on capturing two 12 pdr guns of the RCFA. Lt. H.Z.C. Cockburn sacrificed his command to save them. Later on that day, the Boers made another bid to seize the Canadian guns. Lt. Richard Turner, although wounded, dismounted his men and shouted: "Never let it be said the Canadians had let their guns be taken." Sgt. Eddie Holland protected the left flank with a Colt machine gun. With the Boers almost upon him, he wrenched the red-hot barrel off the carriage, mounted his horse and rode to safety. He received the VC for his bravery, as did Turner and Cockburn.

The Boer War slowly petered out. Early in 1902, a fourth Canadian contingent sailed for South Africa. On March 31, 1902, 22 members of the CMR, serving as rearguard for a large British force, repulsed several hundred Boers at Boschbult, suffering 17 casualties. Days before the war ended in May, four more CMR battalions arrived in South Africa, too late to see action.

Canadians adapted well to conditions in South Africa, gaining a reputation as tough and skilled fighters. Two of them received unique awards. Pvt. R.R. Thompson, a medical orderly, was twice nominated for the VC for going to the aid of wounded soldiers under fire, although he never received the medal. Hearing of this, Queen Victoria knitted a woollen scarf for him and others whose bravery had not been recognized: it is the rarest gallantry decoration ever awarded to a Canadian. A dozen nurses from Canada served in South Africa with British medical units. Georgina Fane Pope, the head nurse, received the Royal Red Cross, the first Canadian to receive this distinction.

Top: Halifax welcomes soldiers returning from the Boer War. AMHC
Bottom: Statue commemorating Canada's contribution to the Boer War in the grounds of Province House, Halifax . JBB

Canada sent 8,372 men to the South African War; 89 died in action, 135 from disease and 252 were wounded. A few weeks after reviewing the RCR at Windsor Castle, Queen Victoria died on January 22, 1901.

The Victorian age ended as the century that Laurier claimed for Canada began. As it dawned in an era of optimism and belief in progress, no one had any inkling of what a terrible hundred years lay ahead.

Top: Nursing Sister Minnie Affleck served with the first Canadian Contingent. DND
Middle: The 1st Canadian Contingent returns. Bottom: The Queen's South African War Medal with campaign bars.

The FIRST WORLD WAR
1914 – 1918
ON LAND

"We had to do what we did. Some died. Some didn't. That's it."
A veteran of Vimy Ridge revisits the battlefield in 1987.

The First World War began with two pistol shots that killed an Austrian archduke and his wife and ended with a sniper's bullet that took the life of a Canadian soldier. Between these two events, nine million soldiers died and millions more returned home wounded in body and mind.

On June 28, 1914, a 19-year-old Serb, Gavrilo Princip, killed Franz Ferdinand, heir to the Austrian throne, in Sarajevo. Within weeks, the European powers mobilized and war began. German troops invaded Belgium, heading for Paris. Britain declared war on Germany on August 4 and brought her empire into the conflict without the approval of the leaders of the countries in it. The "Old Contemptibles" halted the Germans at Mons, and then retreated.

The First World War ended where it began. At eleven in the evening of November 10, 1918, Canadian troops entered Mons. At 10:58 on the following morning, Pvt. George Price from Saskatchewan, a member of the 28th Northwest Battalion, stood in a street of the city holding flowers

Canadian soldiers go over the top. AMHC

given to him by grateful Belgians. A German sniper killed him two minutes before the armistice came into effect.

Canada had no territorial or dynastic ambitions of the kind that lay at the roots of "The Great War". But the sterling performance of her troops in battle paved the way for the country to assert its independence from Britain. Of the 620,000 members of the Canadian Expeditionary Force (CEF), 60,000 died and three times that number were wounded, gassed or injured. The first volunteers, almost half of whom had been born in Britain, expected to be back in Canada by Christmas. Most saw the war as a great adventure. Under the energetic Col. Sam Hughes, Minister of Militia and Defence, an instant army camp arose at Valcartier, near Québec City. Here the First Canadian Division assembled to go overseas. On September 25, 30,617 soldiers began to board troopships. They carried with them the Ross rifle, a weapon manufactured by a friend of Hughes, which later proved useless in battle.

Pvt. James Johnson of the 6th Canadian Mounted Rifles, a unit recruited from four Maritime cavalry regiments, recalled hundreds of people lining the dock at Plymouth, cheering as the Canadians arrived: "It sure made us feel good." By the time the newcomers reached France, the opposing sides had settled into trenches along a 650-km front stretching from the English Channel to the French border.

The Canadians soon established their own style of operation, gaining a reputation for indiscipline – and for daring and initiative in battle. Captain Bernard Montgomery, who would command Canadian troops in the Second World War, found them "a queer crowd lacking soldierly instincts." A British historian ascribed Canadian prowess in war to the "less rigidly hierarchical, less deferential nature of Dominion societies" where officers were promoted on "grounds that had nothing to do with social status." British observers described Canada's soldiers as: "Most wonderful fellows imaginable … The fault with them is that they have no respect for their officers … The Canadian Tommy is in nearly every instance the superior of his British confrères and best of all in attack."

Headquarters, 1 Division, Valcartier Camp and a collection of vehicles. NAC

INTO THE TRENCHES

*"The World wasn't made in a day,
And Eve didn't ride in a bus.
But most of the world's in a sandbag,
And the rest of it's plastered on us"*

Soldiers' song

Canadian troops participated in many battles on the Western Front. They spent most of their time in the trenches, enduring sniping and shelling, taking part in patrols, trench raids and short, sharp attacks on enemy positions. Shelling killed the majority of the troops. Will R. Bird served with the 42nd Battalion (Royal Highlanders of Canada) and wrote *Ghosts Have Warm Hands*. He recalled an officer who refused to believe how close the Germans were and stuck his head over the parapet. Bird shouted, "Don't" – but it was too late. A sniper's bullet drilled a hole in the officer's head.

One soldier wrote: "I don't suppose there is any place on earth in quite such a mess as the surface of the earth surrounding Ypres. For over six miles in depth, the land is nothing but shell-craters, the majority of which are full of water."

The soldier-artist, Paul Nash, described life in the line: "The rain drives on, the stinking mud becomes evilly yellow … the roads and tracks are covered with inches of slime, the black dying trees ooze and sweat and the shells never cease … It is unspeakable, godless, hopeless."

The Allied commanders wanted their troops to take the offensive, and viewed trenches simply as resting places between assaults. The Germans built strong positions with well-equipped dug-outs. Their troops waited out artillery barrages, emerging to mow down attacking troops with machine-guns.

In the Allied trenches, the front edge, the parapet, stood about three metres high and was topped with sandbags. At the rear of the trench, the parados consisted of sandbags. Into the walls of the trenches, the troops dug "funk holes" and dug-outs, where

A soldier crouches as a shell explodes.

After the battle.

they rested and slept. Behind this forward position, communication trenches snaked back to support and reserve lines. On the front of the parapet, rolls of barbed wire protected the line. From firing steps wedged into the parapet soldiers scanned the terrain in front of them. Officers and men crouched here in listening posts, alert to any sign of enemy activity. The order "Stand To!", given at dawn and dusk, brought troops alert as they waited for an enemy attack. If nothing happened, everyone relaxed at the order "Stand Down!". The soldiers sat, smoked, ate, wrote letters and longed for home.

In winter the ground froze – and so did the troops. In summer, life became mired in mud and the dug-outs turned into dark and fetid places. Troops sloshed through the winding trenches, up to their knees in water. The smells of putrefaction, picric acid from shells and disinfectant suffused the lines and rats ran around in the dug-outs. The troops slept in their clothes, their shirts swarming with lice, known as "cooties" or "seam squirrels". Eating canned food and drinking heavily chlorinated water, the soldiers developed skin and stomach diseases. Prolonged immersion in water caused "trench foot". The men groused about the "brass hats" – the senior officers – but endured, relishing the comradeship that made the misery acceptable, hoping to "cop a Blighty"; a wound serious enough to take them out of this insane situation. Men became fatalistic, bidding farewell to their comrades before going over the top in attacks. And they died stoically. Bird heard a man call his name and found a friend lying on a stretcher. "Do you think I've got mine?" he whispered. Bird replied he thought he had and asked if he could do anything for his friend. The man asked for water and Bird brought him some. Then his friend spoke: "Thank you for telling me, I can get myself ready". Bird stayed with his comrade until he "went to sleep".

What made men go on in such conditions? "You just got sort of stupefied", one soldier reported. "You went on with your work and never noticed anything". Canadian veterans retained sharp memories of trench life: "There was a good sense of humour in the war. It's hard to describe. It had a quality of its own, destroying despair and sparking hope." An officer recalled "the golden-heartedness and iron endurance of comrades." Another soldier noted that in the trenches, men felt "larger than life."

Soldiers took little comfort from the message from the old colonial soldier, Lord Roberts, in the "Active Service" Testament

An officer gives a wounded soldier tea, Hill 70. AMHC

issued in 1914: "I ask you to put your trust in God. He will watch over you and strengthen you. You will find in this little Book guidance when you are in health, comfort when you are in sickness and strength when you are in adversity."

Canadian soldiers developed great respect for the padres who went into the front lines with them. Before an attack at Second Ypres in 1915, Canon Frederick Scott, the much-loved senior chaplain of the 1st Canadian Division, stood with the troops of two battalions of the Montreal Scottish as they waited to go into the attack. He recalled that a "great storm of emotion swept through me and I prayed for our men in their awful charge, for I knew that the Angel of Death was passing down our lines that night."

Men facing daily death became prey to superstition. Greg Clark of the 4th Canadian Mounted Rifles won the Military Cross at Vimy. He stood only a metre and a half tall – "exactly the right size for trench warfare" – and carried talismens with him: well-rubbed coins, a nail from a horseshoe, a stone with a hole in it and a pocket New Testament. The daily tot of rum warmed men shivering in the trenches. When they came out of the line and went into rest billets, they scoffed egg and chips and other delicacies offered by the estaminets, locally run cafés. The Salvation Army and the YMCA ran canteens and sought to keep Canadian soldiers on the straight and narrow. But many frequented brothels tolerated by the army.

The Victoria Cross, Britain's highest award for bravery: 633 were awarded in the First World War, 187 of them posthumously. Canadians won four VCs in the Boer War, and 94 VCs in the two world wars.

INTO THE BATTLE

"We might have looked like a ragtag bunch, but we had real discipline. We heard in school about the Thin Red Line, and wondered how well we'd do in battle. After we went into action we realized that we were better than we ever thought we were."

Gunner Murdock MacPhee

The members of the CEF marched into the torn land in early 1915. The core of the Canadian Army consisted of the small Permanent Force. It included the Royal Canadian Dragoons, Lord Strathcona's Horse, the Royal Canadian Regiment, Royal Canadian Horse Artillery, Royal Canadian Garrison Artillery and support arms and services for engineering, ordnance, medical services, etc. The South African War provided a training ground for the Canadian Army. Of its 106 generals in the First World War, at least 34 had served in that conflict. Hamilton Gault, who had served in South Africa, donated $100,000 to raise a regiment of Canadian and British ex-soldiers. The Princess Patricia's Canadian Light Infantry arrived in France in December 1914. It fought under British command until becoming part of the Canadian Corps in 1915. Members of the Princess Pat's gained a reputation for aggressiveness as it sent fighting patrols into "No Man's Land" and enemy trenches. In the first three months of 1915, the regiment suffered 288 casualties, including Lt. Col. Francis Farquhar, the commanding officer, killed by a sniper on March 20.

The Ypres Salient in which the Canadians found themselves lay east of the city. The Germans shelled Ypres into rubble and attacked the Allied troops from three sides.

In mid-April, 1915, the 2nd and 3rd Canadian Infantry Brigades relieved French troops near St. Julien in the salient. A Canadian officer described the trenches they occupied as "being in a deplorable state and in very filthy condition". The Canadians spent five days cleaning them up, deepening them and strengthening the parapets. On April 22, Brigadier-General Arthur Currie, commander of the 2nd Brigade, heard the sound of wagons and gun carriages moving

No Man's Land. AMHC

THE WESTERN FRONT 1914 - 1918

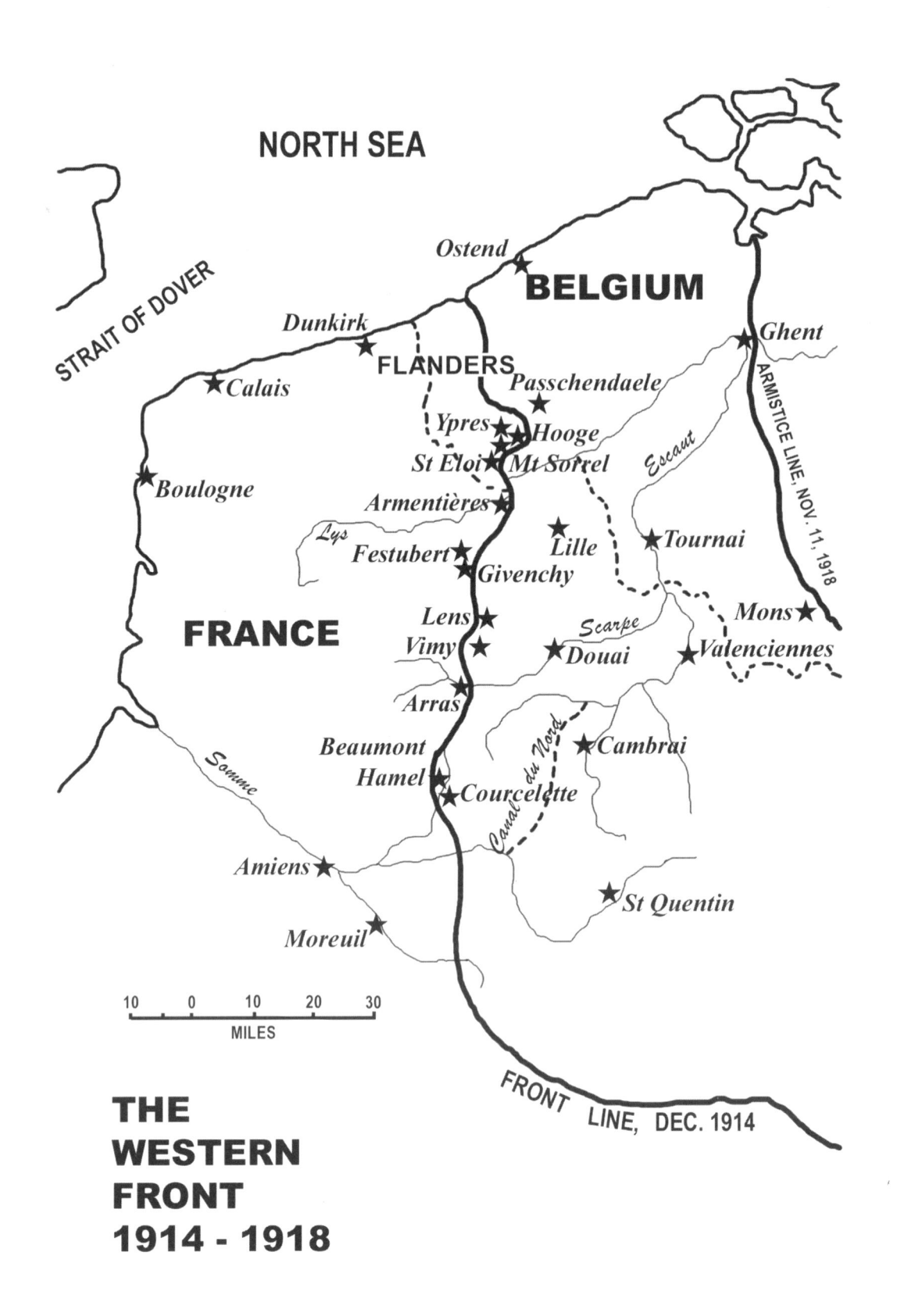

along the German lines opposite his position. In the late afternoon, the Germans released 150 tonnes of chlorine gas. The cloud drifted towards the French lines, its greenish-yellow vapour tearing at the lungs, eyes, noses and throats of the soldiers. Behind the gas came masked German infantry and the French line broke, opening an 8,000 metre gap in the Allied position. The 3rd Canadian Brigade swung around to face the enemy. Nearby, Lt. Col. George Nasmith, a Canadian analytical chemist, and Capt. Francis Scrimger, a medical officer, recognized the gas: "It looks like chlorine and I bet it is." Scrimger moved among the Canadian soldiers, telling them to "urinate on your pocket handkerchief and tie it over you mouth." This turned the gas into crystals, saving many lives. One veteran recalled the gas drifting over them, then seeing the advancing Germans: "They came slowly, thinking we were all dead from the gas, but not so."

The Canadian line held, and by evening the German advance had been halted: Two platoons of the 13th (Montreal) Battalion fought to the last man. Two battalions of the Canadian Scottish attacked Kitchener's Wood, driving the enemy from it and

Gas shells burst in No Man's Land. AMHC

recapturing a British howitzer battery. Next day, the ten officers and 450 survivors of the attack reported at roll call. A British doctor told of long lines of blinded Canadian soldiers led by a man in front who could see. Second Ypres cost the Canadians 2,000 dead and thousands more wounded. L/Cpl. "Bud" Fisher took his Colt machine gun forward under heavy fire to cover the retreat of a gun battery. He died in the front line and his body was never found. He became the first native-born Canadian to win the VC in the war. Francis Scrimger won the medal on April 25 for evacuating the wounded under fire; he survived the war.

The Germans attacked on April 24, driving a wedge into the lines of the 2nd Brigade, then charging the 3rd Brigade position. This time they did not use gas, and the Canadians fell back in good order to the rear and stopped the enemy advance.

Sir John French, the British commander, summed up the achievements of the Canadians at Second Ypres: "In spite of the danger to which they were exposed, they held their ground with a magnificent display of tenacity and courage." On May 6, a shell killed Lt. Alexis Helmer of the Canadian Field Artillery. His friend, Major John McCrae performed the burial service. Deeply affected, he wrote *In Flanders Fields*, the most famous poem of the First World War.

Until the last stages of the war, the Canadian Army consisted of volunteers. Recruiters welcomed Indians, but debarred blacks who sought to enlist, reflecting the prejudice of the time that claimed they would not make good fighters. The 106th (Nova Scotia Rifles) recruited 16 black soldiers. One of them, Jerry Jones, serving with the Royal Canadian Regiment, wiped out a machine gun post at Vimy. Only one black Canadian secured a commission. Rev. William White, the son of slaves, attended Acadia University in Nova Scotia and served as a chaplain. Pressure to recruit black soldiers resulted in the formation of No. 2 Construction Battalion at Pictou, Nova Scotia, July 5, 1916. Officered by whites, the unit did valuable work in and behind the lines.

The Allied generals wanted their men to go over the top to attack German trenches

Soldiers blinded by gas wait to be treated. AMHC.

Canadian gunners in action. AMHC

in set-piece battles. Canadian soldiers suffered grievously from this strategy until their own generals devised better and less costly ways of taking German positions. Before battles began, the soldiers waited in the trenches, alone with their own thoughts. They made sure that their bayonets fitted tightly, that extra ammunition could be easily reached and that their steel helmets fitted properly.

respirator, goggles, a ground flare and a filled water bottle often containing something other than water. So burdened, the soldiers did not charge, but stumbled over the shell-torn land across which German machine-guns sent swathes of bullets.

In the sandbagged pits behind the lines, artillerymen ran up their guns and loaded them before the soldiers attacked. They checked the range one last time. Then the layer, who fired the piece, stood with lanyard in hand, an officer counted down the last seconds, then shouted "Fire." In the early days of the war, gunfire preceded attacks, giving the enemy ample warning. Later troops advanced behind creeping barrages. Will R. Bird tells of a "flying pig" that

Company and platoon commanders, revolvers in hand, whistles in their mouths, glanced nervously at the luminous dials on their wrist watches, hearts thumping as the minutes ticked past. Then they led their men into battle. Each soldier carried about 30 kgs – rifle and bayonet, 120 rounds of ammunition, two Mills bombs, five sandbags, rations for two days, a waterproof sheet,

Three black soldiers in a captured German dugout during the last days of the war. NAC exploded as it left a gun, shredding three men into fragments. With his comrades he picked up the pieces and placed them in sandbags: "It was a harsh breaking-in. We did not say a word as we worked."

The British invented tanks as a way of breaking out of trench warfare. They proved to be clumsy and unreliable monsters. Raymond Brutinel grasped the essence of future wars, and raised a motorized machine-gun unit for mobile warfare. Field Marshal Kitchener dismissed it as "difficult to employ" claiming that it would "throw out of balance the firepower of a division." The Canadian persisted with his innovative ideas, mounting machine-guns on light vehicles and mortars on trucks. Before the Battle of Mount Sorrel in June 1916, Brutinel planned to go on leave. He decided to stay and fight, taking his machine-gunners, plugging a gap in the lines and refusing to withdraw when ordered. Lt. Gen. Sir Julian Byng, the British commander of the Canadians, demanded an explanation. Brutinel provided one then went back to fight with this men, noting that it was a good way to spend his leave. Byng asked another officer: "What sort of fools have we got here?" Brutinel said he was only doing what any other Canadian officer would have done. A letter in the Liddle Collection at the University of Leeds in England, dated May 11, 1918, tells of a Canadian officer who refused to wear his Distinguished Service Order (DSO) "because he was simply doing his job" when he won it. This attitude became pervasive among Canadian soldiers. They sought to defeat the Germans, finish the job that began in 1914 and return home. Lacking a strong military tradition, Canadian leaders and their men had to learn on the job. One writer noted

The beginning of mobile mechanized warfare.
Brigadier Raymond Brutinel's men mount their armoured vehicles. AMHC

27

that as the leader of a national contingent, Currie, when he became a commander of the Canadian Corps, "had a degree of power and influence vastly greater than that of any corps commander from the mother country." And he used this power to secure more resources and to save the lives of his soldiers, preferring to pay for victory in shells rather than in bodies. On May 20, 1915, Currie was ordered to take a German position near Festubert. The men died in hundreds, caught up on the barbed wire in front of the enemy positions. Currie ascribed the failure of the attack to the lack of reconnaissance and preparation. A second attack captured a stretch of German trench. Then British commanders demanded the Canadians mount another assault. Currie planned this attack carefully, ensuring that guns cut the barbed wire before his troops advanced. Two battalions took the Germans positions in half an hour on May 24, for the loss of 53 officers and 1,200 men.

The bravery of the Canadian troops and the skills of their commanders gained them a reputation as "perhaps the most powerful, cohesive corps in the British Expeditionary Force as well as the most tactically and technically innovative," in the words of a

The ruined Cloth Hall in Ypres. It has now been rebuilt and houses a museum. AMHC

leading British military historian.

Bravery meant nothing when generals sent men against machine-guns, as the Battle of the Somme demonstrated. On July 1, 1916, British and French troops rose out of their trenches and moved towards the enemy lines. The British suffered 60,000 casualties on that day, including 20,000 dead, the greatest one-day loss in the country's military history. Among the dead were 310 members of the Newfoundland Regiment. At that time, the colony did not form part of Canada. Its regiment had covered the retreat of the Allied Forces from Gallipoli in January 1916. On July 1, the Newfoundlanders went into action at Beaumont Hamel, dashing across 250 metres of bullet-swept ground to reach their front line trenches. Then they advanced towards the enemy line, making for gaps in the barbed wire. The German machine gunners caught them there and scores died near the "Danger Tree". The attack lasted half an hour "because dead men can advance no further" as their commander said, and no ground was won. During the First World War, the Royal Newfoundland Regiment lost a quarter of its members killed or wounded.

And still the Allied commanders persisted with the same methods of attack against well-entrenched German positions. In February 1917, they ordered Byng, the Canadian commander, to take Vimy Ridge. He organized the assault with care and precision. At the age of 88, James Buchanan summarized the battle in which he fought in one word: "Hellish". As the Canadians dug in, they came across the bodies of British and French soldiers who had died in earlier assaults: "You couldn't put down a shovel but you'd hit a corpse," Buchanan recalled. Vimy Ridge, stretching for six kilometres, rises to a mere 150 metres. The Germans thought their defences would be impregnable. Three lines with endless

---

Top: General Sir Arthur Currie, Commander of the Canadian Corps and one of the best generals of the First World War. AMHC Bottom: The Danger Tree on the Beaumont Hamel Battlefield still stands. JBB

rows of barbed wire in between, scores of machine-guns and numerous gun pits lay in front of the attackers.

For the first time, the four Canadian divisions would fight together. Tunnels led up to the front lines. Here soldiers waited for the attack, chatting, sitting silent, checking their weapons, carving their names, regimental badges and maple leaves into the chalk walls. On the night before the attack, rain and sleet fell. In the early hours of Easter Monday, April 9, the guns in the Souchez Valley and elsewhere opened up and at 5:30 the four divisions went over the top. One soldier recalled that the driving sleet slanted toward the enemy lines blinding the Germans as the Canadians advanced behind creeping barrages. Reaching the first line, the troops cut down the startled sentries and bombed dug-outs, as machine-gunners and infantry opened up on the advancing mass. Individual soldiers worked their way around strong points, killed the gunners and swarmed into the trenches. Then the Canadians surged towards the third set of entrenchments. By mid-morning, members of the 25th Nova Scotia Rifles reached the

The view from the summit of Vimy Ridge. AMHC

The Canadian Monument on Vimy Ridge. JBB Inset: The unveiling of the monument in 1936. DND
The Military Medal was awarded to non-commissioned officers and men. Instituted in 1916, it is the equivalent of the Military Cross awarded to officers.

31

ruins of Thélus, a village near the crest of the ridge.

Four Canadians won the VC at Vimy.

Thain MacDowell, a captain in the 38th (Ottawa) Battalion studied aerial photos and maps before the battle to identify his objectives. In the chaos of the attack, he found himself facing a machine-gun – with only two of his men. MacDowell knocked it out with a hand grenade and charged another one, whose gunner fled. Then the officer ducked into a dug-out and confronted 77 members of the Prussian Guard. He bluffed them into surrender by calling back to an imaginary force supporting him. Pvt. William Milne of the Canadian Scottish knocked out two German machine-guns and was then killed. L/Sgt Ellis Sifton of the 18th (Western Ontario) Battalion, watched his comrades being mowed down as they attacked the second German line. He charged a machine-gun and killed its crew. He too died on Vimy Ridge. Pvt. John Pattison of the Calgary Battalion performed a similar feat of bravery and survived, only to die two months later near Lens.

As the Canadians reached the top of the ridge, a fresh northwest wind arose and the sun broke through as if to celebrate the Canadian victory. The soldiers dug in, watching the Germans scuttle down the rear slopes of the ridge, helping them on with bursts of Lewis gun fire. The Battle of Vimy Ridge ended on April 12, when soldiers from western Canada captured the "Pimple," a heavily defended position at one end of the ridge. They took two hours – and heavy casualties.

Currie called Easter Monday "the grandest day the Corps ever had" and gave full credit for the only Allied victory in 1917 to his men. The king knighted Currie. Promoted to Lieutenant-General, he took command of the Canadian Corps. A survivor of the battle ascribed its success to "professionalism and common sense." Ten per cent of the Canadian Corps became casualties, with 3,598 killed in action and 7,004 wounded. As one veteran put it: " ...it was a big price to pay to occupy an area six by four miles square."

The Canadians gained a reputation as "storm troopers" who fought fiercely and skillfully under officers who cared for their men. Instead of being drafted into different units as British soldiers were, Canadians always fought alongside their fellow-countrymen. Currie set up specialized engineering units rather than assigning these duties to anyone and everyone as did the British. Canadian officers kept their men informed of what was expected of them, and Currie emphasized manoeuver by sections and platoons, thus giving plenty of scope for small group initiative. Soldiers familiarized themselves with the German positions by examining models of the terrain. Col. Andy McNaughton used engineering principles and new technologies such as

Soldiers building a road in Flanders. AMHC.

wireless, sound ranging and aerial observation to organize counter-battery groups. When German guns fired, observers pinpointed their location and Canadian gunners wiped them out. At the Battle of Amiens, Gunner McPhee recalled, the Canadians had "a pretty damn skillful shoot. We did not have to register our guns to check whether we were hitting the target. It was all laid out for us on the map, along with the ranges."

Members of the Canadian Army Medical Corps paid particular attention to ensuring that the wounded survived. The soil of Flanders had been fertilized by human and animal waste for centuries. Shell bursts blew metal into mud-saturated clothes. Men with minor wounds died from gas gangrene from bacteria in the polluted soil. By 1917, blood transfusions began to save lives. One soldier, expected to die, recovered after a transfusion, much to the surprise of the medical officers. Canadian nurses worked in hospitals a few kilometers behind the lines. One reported: "…we three girls had 291 operations in ten nights." About 2,400 nurses went overseas with the CEF and served in England, France, Belgium, Egypt, Greece and Russia in base hospitals, clearing stations, ambulance trains and hospital ships. In all, 47 Canadian nursing sisters lost their lives, including 14 who drowned after the hospital ship *Llandovery Castle* sank after being torpedoed on June 27, 1918, 200 kms off the coast of Ireland.

Constant shelling created a new condition as men began to shiver and shake. Some officers refused to recognize shell shock, especially when the accumulated terror of war made soldiers quit their posts. After the Battle of the Somme in 1916, the commander of the Van Doos had five of his men shot for indiscipline and illegal absence – as an example to the others. The Canadian Army followed the British practice of putting those who fled the trenches in front of a firing squad. The Australians refused to do so, but 22 Canadians ended their lives this way, accused of desertion. In April 1917, mutinies broke out in the French Army and the men of 68 divisions refused to go back into the line. This threw more strains on the Canadian Corps, which had gained an excellent reputation in battle and received more arduous and difficult tasks. On August 15, 1917, Canada's soldiers seized Hill 70, another allegedly impregnable German position, near Lens. Over the next eight

Nurses from No. 7 Stationery Hospital, staffed by Dalhousie University, Halifax. AMHC

Passchendaele. The 16 Canadian Machine Gun Company holds the line. Only Pvt. Ronald Le Brun (foreground) survived. NAC.

days, they held it against 35 counter-attacks in what Currie called "the hardest battle in which the Corps had participated". At Hill 70, the Canadians suffered 8,000 casualties.

Then came Passchendaele.

The soldier-poet, Siegfried Sassoon, summed up this futile battle:

"I died in hell –
(They called it Passchendaele);
my wound was slight
And I was hobbling back, and then a shell
Burst slick upon the duck-board; so I fell
Into the bottomless mud, and lost the light".

General Douglas Haig launched the attack to capture German submarine bases at Zeebrugge and Ostend. The British commander believed that if Passchendaele Ridge were taken, the cavalry would chase the Germans out of Belgium. Against the advice of his engineers, Haig ordered a massive preliminary barrage to soften up German positions. These consisted of concrete pillboxes surrounded by barbed wire. The shells turned the ground into one vast quagmire. Gunner McPhee with the 36th (Howitzer) Battery described the battlefield as "Mud. Mud. Mud." He recalled how the horses would "lay into the traces and breast collars" yet fail to move the guns through the clinging mire. Gunners grabbed the drag ropes, while others put their shoulders to the wheels to ensure that the attacking infantry would have artillery support.

The Canadians went into battle on October 26 under a blood-red sky. Major Talbot Papineau left a staff job to join the Princess Pat's. Before he went over the top, he turned to another officer and said, "You know, Hughie, this is suicide." A shell burst killed him. Papineau was one of the 750 dead his regiment lost at Passchendaele. The Edmonton Regiment lost 443 officers and men out of 588 in the battle. "Hoodoo" Kinross survived – and won the VC. A disaster on parade, he proved to be a fierce fighter, outflanking a machine-gun and killing the gunners.

Arthur Hickson of the 25th (New Brunswick) Battalion expected its attack on November 6 to be a "nonchalant stroll through enemy lines". Shells falling into the muddy terrain showered soldiers with mud rather than shrapnel. As the New Brunswickers advanced, four of the five officers in Hickson's company fell. A sergeant, shot in both legs, used his rifle to pull himself forward. Hickson threw a bottle of rum that he carried to him. Much to Hickson's surprise, the other man took only a hefty swig before sending the bottle back. The Canadians dropped into shell holes and began to link them up to form trenches. The mud clung to their shovels and water poured into their hastily constructed positions.

Soldier Pioneers carry forward duckboards in the morass of the Passchendaele battlefield. NAC

Will R. Bird's platoon relieved men who seemed to be half-drunk in a dry sector of the battlefield. Someone reported seeing Germans in front of the position. Bird went out with an officer to investigate. A flare went up and they spotted a line of enemy helmets. Creeping forward they found only dead men, killed by shrapnel and beginning to decompose. After a failed attack on a pillbox, Bird saw a sniper shoot a stretcher-bearer tending a wounded man. With two of his comrades he killed the German.

As Bird put it, no man who endured Passchendaele would ever be the same again, and would "forever be a stranger to himself." Another soldier noted: "We had won the ridge, but lost the battalion." Currie forecast 16,000 Canadian casualties. The total losses of the Canadian Corps came to 15,654.

In 1917, it looked as if the Allies might lose the war. As the Battle of Passchendaele ground on, the Austrians and Germans attacked in Northern Italy and the Italian army collapsed at Caporettto. Lenin and the Bolsheviks seized power in Russia on November 7 and prepared to take their country out of the war. The German High Command began to transfer their troops from the Eastern to the Western Front. German submarines practised unrestricted warfare, sinking any ship taking supplies to Britain. The United States declared war on April 6, but had to train her troops before they could be sent into combat. In April, just over 3,000 Canadians volunteered to serve in a month with 13,232 casualties. Against objections from Québec, conscription became law in Canada on August 29, although the first call-up did not take place until January 1918.

On March 21, 1918, "The Kaiser's Battle" began as 64 German divisions swarmed across the fields of Flanders. Small groups of experienced soldiers probed weak spots in the enemy lines, bypassing strong-points. The Germans advanced 40 km from their start line, taking thousands of prisoners as the British Fifth Army crumbled.

On March 30, Lt. Gordon Flowerdew led three troops of Lord Strathcona's Horse from his under strength squadron at full gallop towards the Germans in the Bois de Moreuil, near Amiens. Cut down by

---

Top: A crucifix still stands in a ruined land. AMHC
Middle: Hill 70 after Canadian shelling. AMHC
Bottom: Victorious Canadians show off some of their loot. AMHC

The Charge of Flowerdew's Squadron, by Sir Alfred Munnings. LDSH

enemy fire, the cavalrymen broke the enemy line, losing three quarters of their strength. Flowerdew fell, but continued to cheer on his men. He died of his wounds, receiving a posthumous VC.

Brutinel's Machine Gun Brigade moved quickly to areas threatened by the German advance. One veteran recalls saying goodbye and shaking hands with his comrades as each vehicle went into battle – something they had never done before. On March 24, one battery lost 42 of its 50 members while covering a British retreat. On the following day, two Canadian armoured cars and six scouts on motorcycles caught German troops crossing the Somme. They killed scores of them and dispersed the rest without suffering any losses.

The German soldiers outran their supply lines and became more interested in looting than in fighting. The Allies rallied and began to push them back.

On August 8, 1918 what became known as "Canada's Hundred Days" began.

With Australian and British troops, Currie's men began the final push at Amiens. The war became even more vicious and men went into battle shouting: "Remember the Llandovery Castle." A Canadian colonel told his men that he could not order them not to take prisoners, noting that "if you take any we'll have to feed' em out of your rations". At the Battle of Amiens, troops found German guns whose muzzle caps had not been removed. Their crews lay nearby – dead. One battalion captured a regimental headquarters and found the general's porridge still warm. Hundreds of Germans tried to surrender but were cut down. On August 8, three Canadian divisions, supported by over 100 tanks and air power advanced almost 14 km. Casualties totalled 4,109 including 1,306 dead. The Canadians destroyed two German divisions, took over 5,000 prisoners and won four more VCs.

Then they smashed through the Drocourt-Quéant Line, with the help of tanks bearing maple leaves, winning another seven VCs. Currie mounted a brilliant attack on the Canal du Nord, and the Canadians took the ruined city of Cambrai.

The Germans fought a savage rearguard action. On November 10, a strange silence

---

Canadian gunners with two pieces mounted on sledges for the Russian campaign. AMHC

settled over the battlefields. Gunner MacPhee recalled "a feeling that things were going to end. It didn't seem dramatic when it did on the next day." The men in Will R. Bird's platoon relaxed and talked about what they would do in the future. It never came for some of them. The Company Sergeant Major told the soldiers they had to capture Mons: "Orders are orders." Bird's men relieved members of the Princess Pat's under fire from machine-guns and artillery. A shell killed two men near Bird, and he knocked out a German machine-gun with a rifle grenade.

And then his war ended. But it continued for Canadian soldiers and airmen who volunteered to serve against the "Bolos" in Russia. Veterans of the Western Front landed at Murmansk and Archangel, and the 16th Brigade, Canadian Field Artillery distinguished itself on Dvina Front. About 5,000 Canadians served in the Siberian Expeditionary Force. Major Peter Anderson commanded an armoured train that smashed a Red offensive. In Vladivostock, Canadians co-operated with Japanese and Americans, training anti-Bolshevik forces and guarding huge quantities of supplies sent by the Allies. Others served with Dunsterforce in Northern Persia. But the Canadian government had no interest in supporting those seeking to preserve the old order in Russia, and ordered the troops home. Six Mounties, under Farrier Sergeant Margetts, took some of their horses across the country to hand over to White Russians. Bolsheviks derailed their train. The Mounties fought back and drove them off. By the fall of 1919, all Canadian troops had left what one of them recalled as a "nasty, filthy, cold blooded country."

Canada's servicemen and women earned, and retain to this day, the unstinting admiration of those with whom they served in the First World War. In January 1999, the French government decorated the remaining survivors of the conflict with the Légion d'Honneur. The magnificent performance of her troops in battle secured Canada her own seat at the table during the discussions about the peace treaty.

One veteran recalled an incident illustrating the typical modesty of Canadians: "At the end of the [war] the Yanks were parading through a small village in France and they had a big sign: 'WE WON THE WAR!' Behind them came the Canadians with a smaller sign: 'WE HELPED!'"

The Distinguished Service Order, awarded only to officers.

IN THE AIR

"They are the knighthood of the air, without fear, without reproach and they recall the legendary days of chivalry, not merely by the daring of their exploits but by the nobility of their spirit."

Prime Minister Lloyd George of Britain (1917).

As the war in the trenches ground on and soldiers hurled themselves at the enemy and died in their thousands, the public in the warring powers sought heroes. They found them in the skies above the battlefields. These airmen seemed to have recaptured a nobler style of battle, based on single combat, fought between individuals in the infinity of the heavens. Many cavalry officers, finding themselves bogged down in the mud of Flanders instead of gaily charging enemy lines, transferred to the Royal Flying Corps (RFC) and the Royal Naval Air Service (RNAS). Among them was Billy Bishop. When an airman shot down five planes, he became an "ace," a word coined by the French. Bishop destroyed 72 enemy aircraft, becoming the second highest Allied scorer. As one writer put it, this Canadian pilot "epitomized everything that the public demanded of a Knight of the Air. Young, dashing and handsome, he exuded an appealing mixture of gentlemanly manners and schoolboy deviltry."

William Avery Bishop from Owen Sound disliked authority and formal learning, but behaved brilliantly in battle. While growing up, he shot squirrels with deadly accuracy and carried the ability as a marksman into his life as a combat pilot. Bishop's school principal told his parents that "the only thing your son is good for is fighting." At Royal Military College the young man gained a reputation as a rebellious brawler and ladies' man. Considered the worst cadet at the college, Bishop narrowly escaped expulsion just as the war began. Barging into a recruiting office, he demanded to join "whatever outfit is going over first" and immediately became a lieutenant in the Mississauga Horse.

Arriving in Britain in the summer of 1915, Bishop found himself in the "military hell" of Shorncliffe Camp. One day a fighter plane landed nearby after the pilot became lost. Up to his knees in mud and soaked to the skin, Bishop made a decision. Turning

No. 1 and No. 2 Fighter Squadrons, Canadian Air Force came into being on November 17–20, 1918. DND

A bewildering array of machine guns on a BE2, First World War fighter. SAM.

to his companion in misery, he said: "George, it's clean up there...If you died at least it would be a clean death." Bishop transferred to the RFC, received his wings in 1916 and shot down his first plane, an Albatross, on March 25, 1917.

Although encouraged to do so by the British commanders, Canada did not form its own air force in the First World War. Some 22,000 Canadians joined the RFC or the RNAS, including Lester B. Pearson, a future prime minister. In all, 3,135 Canadian flyers won their wings – and 1,388 of them died in combat, accidents or from other causes. The life expectancy of these young men lasted from three to six weeks.

To become a pilot in Britain, you had to be "an officer and a gentleman." As colonials, Canadians did not have to respect the constraints of the British class system. A flight surgeon claimed that the Canadians had an advantage, as these outdoorsmen had not been coddled like his fellow British! Canadians proved to be outstanding flyers and fighters, providing 11 of the top 27 aces from Britain and its empire who downed more than 30 enemy planes each.

The first airmen went aloft in flimsy craft that often proved more dangerous to them than to the enemy. In the early days of the war, planes from both sides took aerial photographs, spotted for gunners, reported troop movements and dropped small bombs or fléchettes (steel darts) on enemy lines. Observers sat behind or in front of the pilot, manning machine-guns and engaging in aerial combat. Some planes went down in flames, for their wings and fuselages were covered in canvas saturated with highly combustible dope. If a pilot turned his plane too quickly in the air, it could plunge into the ground while the wings of others simply fell off the fuselage: more pilots died in accidents than in combat. Flyers did not carry parachutes, considering them an affront. The Allied commanders insisted that "a pilot's job is to stick to his aeroplane."

By 1916, the Allies commanded the skies. As planes became more sophisticated and faster, they still retained their role as platforms for aerial surveillance rather than as fighting machines. Then "Tony" Fokker, a young Dutchman working in Germany, invented a device for firing a machine-gun through a plane's propeller without shredding it. A new era in aerial warfare began. A pilot pointed his plane at an enemy one, pulled a trigger and riddled it with bullets. The concept of the "fighter" – the scout – had arrived.

Billy Bishop took to this new form of fighting with characteristic zeal and enthusiasm. On March 31, 1917, he returned from an escort mission in his Nieuport Scout

VC winners Billy Bishop and William Barker in front of a D.VII at Leaside, near Toronto, in 1919.
K.M. Molson Collection

and filed a report: "While on escort, I went to the assistance of another Nieuport being attacked by an Albatross Scout. I opened fire twice, the last time at 50 yards range, my tracers were seen to hit his machine in the center section. Albatross seemed to fall out of control, as he was in a spinning nosedive with his engine on. Albatross crashed at 7:30: Ref 51B.29-30."

than a third of their fighters. Bishop proved to be a reckless pilot, but shot down four enemy aircraft and two balloons during this period. Known as the "Lone Hawk," he followed his own individualistic way of aerial combat. On June 2, Bishop took off alone, attacked a German aerodrome and shot down three Albatrosses. On his return, he congratulated the station armourer for

Then came "Bloody April".

The Germans, with superior fighters, flew in mutually supportive formations, choosing the time and place of their attacks. Major General Sir Hugh Trenchard, commander of the RFC, ordered his squadron leaders to take the offensive, to seek out and attack the enemy wherever they found him. This policy provided disastrous. Between April 4 and 8, the British lost 75 aircraft in combat and another 56 in accidents – more

keeping his Vickers machine-gun in good firing condition. For this feat, Bishop won a VC to add to the DSO and MC he received from the King, the only known occasion when all three medals were presented at the same time. One of his fitters "souvenired" his flying helmet: it now resides in a box in the Liddle Collection.

Bishop, a man of quick impulses, was looked upon by his squadron mates he noted, "like some sort of wild man from the zoo."

Morane Parasol. AMHC

But he wrote: "I had found the one thing I loved above all others. To me it was not a business or a profession, but just a wonderful game" – albeit a deadly one.

About half of the Canadians who flew overseas came from urban areas, and a third of them hailed from Toronto. Many had been white-collar workers or students with an average age of around 20. As the casualties mounted through the dreary days of 1917 and 1918, the public revelled in stories of the deeds of the knights of the air, unaware of the dull, tense and short lives of many of them.

John Bernard ("Don") Brophy, born in Ottawa in 1893, loved sports and athletics. He flunked his first year at McGill University, learned to fly and left Canada as a second lieutenant in the RFC on December 8, 1915, to train in Britain. In his diary, the young man pondered on the possibility of being "reduced to hash by a collision with the earth". Bumptious, brave and stoical, Brophy piloted an outdated, unstable RE7 over the battlefront. Three times the plane's engine failed while in flight and this "annoyed me to a certain extent." On his first patrol over enemy lines on May 28, 1916, the engine again quit, the plane landed and the undercarriage and the propeller flew off as a wing tip and the nose hit the ground. As Brophy wrote: "The engine proceeded to turn very well without the prop, so I switched off and got out." Brophy walked back to base, tried to start the only serviceable plane, failed to do so, and returned to his quarters.

On July 1, 1916, as the British attacked on the Somme, Brophy bombed the railway and stores at Bapaume. On the next day he dropped 150-kg bombs on a German headquarters, but could see no damage. If

Bristol Scout. AMHC

dropped from above 1,500 metres, these missiles buried themselves in the ground without exploding. After a spell of leave, Brophy chased Zeppelins over Britain. Fighter pilots now had to learn how to twist and turn to avoid the enemy and to attack them. On the afternoon of Christmas Eve, 1916, Brophy took up a BE12 single seater fighter, dived sharply, then looped the loop perfectly. As he turned to land, the plane, strained beyond its limits, spiraled down out of control and hit the ground at 250 km an hour. Don Brophy met the death about which he had mused while in training.

Harold Price, another Canadian flyer, had a very different war. The Torontonian entered the RFC in late 1916, before his 20th birthday. An introspective, puritanical youth brought up in a strict Methodist household, Price loved to fly and hoped to engage in aerial combat in Europe. When he won his wings on May 25, 1917, he went instead with 63 Squadron to Mesopotamia (now Iraq). He fought German pilots flying for the Turks and bombed troops, aerodromes and supply depots between Baghdad and Samarra. In his diary, Price wrote of headaches, fevers, stomach problems – and defective engines. Sandfly fever, heatstroke and other ailments felled 24 officers out of 30, and 130 airmen out of 200, leaving the rest to run the squadron. A storm in April 1918 wrecked their base and planes, doing more damage in two hours than the enemy ever inflicted.

Price bombed and strafed retreating Turkish troops, but when he saw them waiting to surrender, he did not have the heart to machine-gun the men and horses. On June 8, 1918, Price had a "pretty good crash". Both he and his observer walked away from it but the "bus" looked "a most unholy mess." Price fell ill with fever in March 1919, and entered hospital. He survived and later became a doctor.

Billy Bishop also survived the war, as did another Canadian pilot who won the VC. William Barker, also a cavalryman, transferred to the RFC shortly after arriving in France and serving in the Ypres Salient. He became an observer, qualified as a pilot and joined a fighter squadron. Over France he shot down five enemy aircraft in October 1917, then move to Italy to prop up the crumbling Allied front there. By the time he returned to England as an instructor in September 1918, Barker had gained a reputation as an "artist with a pair of Vickers". On October 27, Barker took off from England in a Sopwith Snipe for "one last look at the war," and shot down a German two-seater. Then a Fokker triplane jumped him, its bullets shattering his right leg. Fainting from pain, Barker lost control of his plane with the enemy in close pursuit. Recovering consciousness, the Canadian turned on his attacker and shot him down. Then 20 other Fokkers pounced on the solitary enemy. Barker quickly shot down three of them – then fainted again. When he came to, he found himself in the middle of 60 German fighters. Wounded in the legs and the arm, Barker shot down several of the enemy planes and fought his way out of the melée. The Snipe took 300 bullets, but somehow he managed to land it inside the British lines. The undercarriage tore away, followed by a part of the wing and the fuselage, but Barker suffered only a broken nose and was rescued by members of the Highland Light Infantry. He spent a week unconscious in a Rouen hospital, awakening to find he had won the VC for his extraordinary feat and his 53 victories.

Alan McLeod won the VC at the age of 18, the youngest person to receive the medal in the First World War. One of the observers who flew with him described the young Canadian as being "devoid of fear." In March 1918, as the Germans mounted their final offensive, McLeod's squadron of Armstrong-Whitworth bombers lumbered off in foul weather to bomb the advancing troops. As McLeod prepared to drop his missiles on a German battery, a red Fokker of Richthofen's Flying Circus attacked his plane. The observer shot it down and then seven more German planes swarmed towards the bomber, setting it on fire and wounding the crew. McLeod eased himself out of the cockpit on to the lower wing, put the plane into a sideslip and blew out the flames as the Fokkers continued their attack. McLeod then crash-landed the plane in a shell hole in No Man's Land. Both McLeod and the observer survived. As the bombs and ammunition exploded in the blazing wreckage, McLeod dragged his companion to safety. South African soldiers found the pilot unconscious, with six wounds, still grasping the collar of his observer. The VC winner returned home to Stonewall, Manitoba, only to die of flu five days before the war ended.

Raymond Collishaw went to sea at the age of 15 and with Scott to the Antarctic in 1911, enlisting in the Royal Naval Air Service in 1916 at the age of 23. Flying with the 3rd Naval Wing, he shot down his first plane on October 12. Early in 1917, as a flight commander, he had parts of his Sopwith triplanes painted black. With four other pilots – Reid, Sharman, Nash and Alexander – he led one of the most successful missions of the entire war in July 1917. The Black Maria, Black Death, Black Sheep, Black Roger and Black Prince downed 67 German planes, with Collishaw accounting for almost half of them. By the end of the war, he had

Major William Barker with wreckage of Sopwith Camel, of No. 28 Squadron, in Italy. NAC

recorded 60 victories. He added another three fighting the Bolsheviks with 47 Squadron. Collishaw then made a fighting retreat to the Black Sea where he watched a tank drive over his squadron's planes to prevent them from falling into the hands of the Reds.

A Canadian downed Germany's most successful air ace, Manfred Von Richthofen, the "Red Baron", named for the colour of his Fokker triplane. By April 15, 1918, he had accumulated 80 kills, the highest total of any First World War ace. On that day, he led a flight of 15 Germans planes into combat with eight British Sopwith Camels. "Wop" May, a newcomer, was flying one of the Camels. His guns jammed, and as ordered, he headed for home. Richthofen, ever alert for easy pickings, attacked May as Roy Brown, the Canadian leading the British flight, flew to the rescue of his companion. He poured fire into the red triplane, which landed with the pilot dead at the controls. A Lewis gun fired by Australian soldiers may have killed the ace. The cause of Richthofen's death is still disputed.

"The Code of the Pilot", published during the war, claimed that: "No honourable aviator attacks an aeroplane that is already on fire. Such a foe has enough trouble to deal with; he is regarded as out of the fight". To war-weary civilians, Billy Bishop and other flyers represented the ideal warrior – not the mud-stained soldiers huddling in fear as enemy guns shredded their comrades. Bishop strafed downed enemy airmen and admitted killing the crew of a plane after the observer's guns jammed. The Germans called Allied pilots "Hell's Handmaidens." In his 1917 book, *Winged Warfare*, Bishop noted how the public loved the "red hot, hurray-for-our side stuff." Later in life he

Sopwith Camel. AMHC

47

found the book so terrible that he could not read it – "It turns my stomach."

For every ace who found fame and glory in the skies above the battlefields, there were a dozen Don Brophys, ordinary men with the courage of early morning. Lacking Bishop's skills and luck, they died in accidents or in flaming aircraft plummeting to earth.

On April 1, 1918, the RFC and RNAS combined to become the Royal Air Force. In November 1918, two all-Canadian units at Upper Heyford, Oxfordshire, formed 1 and 2 Squadrons of the Canadian Air Force. Too late to see combat, the squadrons disbanded in 1920. The Royal Canadian Air Force formally came into being on April 1, 1924.

The Distinguished Flying Cross (with purple stripes) instituted in 1918 and awarded to officers and warrant officers. The Air Force Cross (with red stripes) is awarded for acts of bravery, not necessarily in the face of the enemy.

AT SEA

"Canada's...naval contribution to the World War was so small...that no Canadian naval history need be recorded here."

The Cambridge History of the British Empire (1930).

Laurier's government created the Royal Canadian Navy (RCN) on May 4, 1910. The outbreak of hostilities, however, found the nation woefully unprepared for war at sea.

Many Canadians joined the British Navy. At the Battle of Coronel, off the coast of Chile, on November 1, 1914, HMS *Good Hope* sank, carrying four young Canadian midshipmen with her. The RCN and the Canadian Army rejected Rowland Bourke when he tried to enlist because of his defective eyesight. So he headed for Britain and joined the Royal Naval Voluntary Reserve. On May 10, 1918, he took his motor launch into Ostend harbour during an attempt to block its entrance. Under heavy fire, Bourke rescued three sailors floundering in the water and won the VC.

In 1914, the RCN had only two ancient cruisers in her fleet, HMCS *Niobe* at Halifax and HMCS *Rainbow* at Esquimault, and few trained men. Two submarines acquired from United States yards at a cost of $1.15 million never became operational. On its coastal patrols, HMS *Niobe* kept breaking down so it was docked in Halifax.

As German submarines began to sink schooners, trawlers and other vessels around

---

Devastation on the Halifax waterfront after the December 6 Explosion in 1917. HMCS *Niobe* on right. MCM

Canada's first two submarines – CC1 and CC2 – shown in Esquimault Harbour in 1914. MCM

the coasts of North America, the British Admiralty asked Canada in 1916 to create a naval force to patrol its waters. The captain of U-156 captured *Triumph*, a Canadian trawler, mounted a gun on her and the mini-raider sank six Canadian schooners. U-156 hit a mine off Scotland and sank. German submarines laid mines off Sambro Light and Peggy's Cove but they did not sink any ships.

The RCN did valuable work escorting convoys on the east coast. A number of Canadians served with the Royal Naval Air Service, accounting for five of the seven U-boats sunk by its planes.

On December 6, 1917, the war came to Canada. The explosives-laden French ship *Mont Blanc* and the Belgian relief vessel *Imo* collided in Halifax Harbour just before nine in the morning. The *Mont Blanc* caught fire and her crew abandoned her. As she drifted towards the Halifax shore, sailors from HMCS *Niobe* boarded her and secured hawsers, hoping to tow the blazing vessel away from the shoreline. Here hundreds of people lined up to view the sight. For some it would be their last as the *Mont Blanc*, laden with 2,600 tons of picric acid, gun cotton and TNT exploded in a huge fireball. Every sailor from the *Niobe's* pinnace died as the ship vaporized. Parts of the vessel rained on the old cruiser, knocking down one of her funnels and riddling the upperworks with shrapnel. The Richmond area of North End Halifax, which received the full brunt of the explosion, resembled a battlefield.

By the end of the war, Canada had more than a hundred warships, most of them small, and 7,000 officers and men serving in the RCN. Canada's first air force, the Royal Canadian Naval Air Service, came into being after the government built bases at North Sydney and Eastern Passage, near Dartmouth. Airmen and sailors went to Boston and Britain to train in the summer of 1918, but the war ended before they could see action.

CANADA'S FIRST NATIONS GO TO WAR

"The war proved that the fighting spirit of my tribe was not squelched through reservation life...our people showed all the bravery of our warriors of old."

Mike Mountain House, First World War veteran.

Herded on reserves, governed by a paternalistic bureaucracy, Canada's Indians had no reason to volunteer to serve a country that treated them so shabbily. Yet over 7,000 of them enlisted during the two world wars and the Korean conflict. Over 500 Indians and Métis died while in the services, and about 50 received decorations for bravery.

Lt. Cameron Brant, a descendant of Joseph Brant, died leading a counterattack at Second Ypres, in April 1915. On October 13, 1944, Lt. Victor Moore guided a bulldozer clearing a roadblock near Rimini in Italy, while under shell and small arms fire. He won the Military Cross for his "perseverance and courage." His younger brother, Lloyd George Moore, went down with HMCS *St. Croix*, torpedoed on September 20, 1943.

During the First World War, Indians served as snipers and scouts, two hazardous infantry roles. Cpl. Francis Pegahmagabow won the Military Medal and two bars for his bravery in battle, demonstrating patience

---

Sgt Tommy Prince, a Canadian Indian, won the Military Medal and the American Silver Star during the Second World War and later served in Korea. He is shown here with his brother Morris at his investiture at Buckingham Palace, Feb 12, 1945. NAC

and superb marksmanship. Indians and Métis found it difficult to adapt to military discipline. "Ducky" Norwest, a Métis from Alberta, enlisted in January, 1915, only to be discharged three months later for misbehaviour. Signing up under another name, Norwest became an inspiration to his unit. Pleasant and kindly with his comrades, he showed complete dedication in the line, winning the Military Medal at Vimy Ridge. With an official record of 115 hits, Norwest died three months from the end of the war – killed by a sniper's bullet.

During the Second World War, Tommy Prince became a paratrooper. He won the Military Medal at Anzio with the Canadian-American First Special Service Force ("The Devil's Brigade") and the U.S. Silver Star during the invasion of southern France. Sgt. Prince joined the first Canadian unit, the Princess Pat's, that arrived in Korea in 1950, and saw action with it. He returned for a second tour in 1952, dying in poverty ten years later. At his funeral, a delegation from his old regiment served as pallbearers, and Indians chanted "Death of a Warrior" as drummers beat a lament.

Oliver Martin joined the Haldimand Rifles, a militia unit, as a bugler in 1909, then became a company commander in France and Belgium, surviving a gas attack. Transferring to the Royal Flying Corps, Martin served as an observer in 1917 before earning his pilot's wings in the following year. After the war, he returned to teaching and assumed command of the Haldimand Rifles. During the Second World War, Martin trained hundreds of recruits in Canada before retiring in October 1944 as a brigadier. Other Indians and Métis returned from the wars with new skills to lead their people in a variety of roles. Their military experiences offered them opportunities for learning and achievement lacking on the reserves and in Canadian society. And the memory of their toughness, dedication and commitment inspired others seeking an equal place in the nation for their people.

A young Indian recruit receives her chief's blessing in 1942. NAC

The MOUNTIES' MILITARY TRADITION

"Seamen? I have no seamen except the 'Mounties' and the 'Rummies' they used to chase."

Canadian naval official at the beginning of the Second World War.

The sterling performance of the members of the North West Mounted Police in the South African War and after, and the success of the force in keeping the peace in the west, earned it the designation "Royal" in 1904. When war broke out ten years later, the federal government forbade members of the RNWMP from taking leaves of absence to join the army. About 1,000 members of the force whose term had expired - or who wangled their discharges - became soldiers. Trooper J.H.McBrien received a field commission and rose to the rank of major general. Two Mounties won the Victoria Cross.

Constable George Pearkes served in the Yukon, securing his release in 1915. Enlisting as a private, he became an officer, winning the DSO and the Military Cross. In October 1917, Major Pearkes commanded a company of the 5th Canadian Mounted Rifles. Leading his men in an attack on Vapour Farm amid the mud of Passchendaele, Pearkes felt a piece of shrapnel smash into his thigh. He kept on, securing his objective. "I said to myself, I've got to go on a while, wounded or not," he later said. With a handful of survivors, Pearkes held the position against a German counterattack. Then he had his wound treated. During the Second World War, Pearkes commanded the 1st Canadian Division, served as Minister of National Defence (1957-60) then as Lieutenant Governor of British Columbia (1960-68).

The postwar career of the other Mountie who won the Victoria Cross followed a very different path. Michael O'Leary served in the Irish Guards, immigrated to Canada, and joined the RNWMP. In the fall of 1915 he

A member of the Provost Corps in a ruined French town. NAC

was released to rejoin his old regiment. On February 1, 1915, as his battalion advanced towards German lines, O'Leary charged ahead, killed five of the enemy in a trench then took out a machine-gun crew. Commissioned in the Connaught Rangers, he returned to Canada after the war and joined the Ontario Provincial Police. Then he moved to the United States, became involved in smuggling liquor during Prohibition, and landed in jail. Returning to Britain in 1931, he went back into uniform - as a doorman at the Mayfair Hotel in London. During the Second World War, he served as a captain in the Pioneer Corps.

The redoubtable Sam Steele wanted to lead his men into battle during the First World War. Impressed by the cheerful gallantry of the French Canadians he met while a Mountie, Steele encouraged the formation of the Royal 22è Régiment, the Van Doos. As a major general, Sam Steele trained recruits in Britain, was knighted and died a year later in 1919 during the flu epidemic, at the age of 68.

Towards the end of the war, members of the force were allowed to volunteer, forming "A" squadron of the Canadian Cavalry Brigade in France. Another squadron sought to keep order in Vladivostok, Russia, during the Allied occupation in 1918-19.

A few days after the outbreak of war in 1939, word came from Ottawa that Mounties would not be allowed to volunteer for the Canadian Armed Forces. However, the minister responsible agreed to the formation of a provost company from the Force, and the incorporation of its marine and air divisions into the RCN and the RCAF.

"Skipper" MacNeil, father of Robert MacNeil, formerly of the MacNeil-Lehrer Hour, joined the RCMP Marine Division in 1933. The book-loving officer commanded a Halifax-based patrol ship that chased rumrunners smuggling booze from the U.S. into Nova Scotia. When war broke out, MacNeil found some of these audacious seamen under his command on the corvette HMCS *Dauphin*. It carried a unique crest commissioned by its captain - a Mountie, waving a revolver, riding a German submarine. *Dauphin* rescued the crew of a torpedoed Norwegian ship in a North Atlantic gale, and MacNeil received an award from that country's king for this feat. Like many other corvette sailors, "Skipper" had a hard war, surviving on "gin and cigarettes and the adrenaline of danger," in the words of his son.

While waiting to go into action, members of the Provost Company learned to ride their motor cycles along twisting English country lanes, investigated crimes committed by Canadian soldiers, traced deserters and sought out those who stole military equipment and supplies. In 1943,

Gunshield art on HMCS *Dauphin*, a Canadian corvette captained by "Skipper" MacNeil, a former Mountie. MCM

the provost unit went to Sicily. Here, in Italy and Northwest Europe former Mounties scouted out traffic routes, manned crossroads, directed supply trucks forward, helped to evacuate the wounded and reconnoitered roads and river crossings, often under shell, mortar and machine-gun fire. In all, 213 Mounties served as provost officers. Twelve died in battle or accidents, including Lt. P. Oliver, killed at Dieppe.

The style with which they handled their duties on dangerous roads and kept the troops moving emerges from one report: "Occasional trouble arose with Polish Corps drivers who persisted in going the wrong way on one-way routes, and with the Greeks who thought looting should be permitted. The answers had never been given at Depot Division, Regina, nor were they in any army textbook. They were furnished on the spot, with Provost personnel using tact and persuasion and sometimes more forceful means. And through it all, the roads were kept open and looting to a minimum."

The splendid international reputation of the Mounties ensured their welcome as peacekeepers on UN missions. Cpl. Barry Mellish volunteered for service with UNPROFOR in Croatia in 1992 and 1994 because: "I wanted some adventure - and the chance to serve people elsewhere in the world." Other members of the Force have served in Haiti, the Congo, East Timor and elsewhere. One hundred of them volunteered for the UN Transition Assistance Group in Namibia in 1989. Here they learned to cope with snakes, scorpions, and wild elephants while helping in the new nation's electoral process. One UN official commented: "In their first week, the Mounties did more organizational and public relations work in the communities - both black and white - than the police from other countries did in six months."

Members of the Provost Corps keep the traffic moving after the invasion of Europe. NAC

The SECOND WORLD WAR
1939 – 1945

ON LAND

"Now therefore We do Declare and Proclaim that a State of War with the German Reich exists and has existed in our Dominion of Canada as and from the tenth day of September, 1939."

Canada Gazette, September 10, 1939.

The ever-cautious government of Mackenzie King declared a policy of "limited liability" in the first month of the war. The nation would fight the enemy with volunteers. Canadians would serve all over the world in the next six years, from Alaska to Germany. They would endure boredom in Britain while waiting to go into action - and die in hundreds in futile battles in Hong Kong and Dieppe. The government would again introduce conscription, against opposition in Québec and send conscripts to fight in Europe, despite promises that it would not do so.

The outbreak of war found the country unprepared. The army had only 4,000 soldiers and 16 light tanks, the navy a small fleet of ships and the air force a single squadron of Hurricane fighters. By the time peace came, almost a million Canadians had served in uniform, about ten per cent of the population. And 42,042 had died in the service of Canada, while thousands of others returned home wounded.

In September, 54,884 men enlisted, but the services refused to recruit women. Geraldine Turcotte wanted to join up "the

---

The government sold saving stamps and showed how much a 25 cent one bought.

58

minute war was declared... But they weren't ready for women in 1939." She eventually became one of the 17,000 members of the Royal Canadian Air Force (Women's Division): "We were made to understand that we were recruited so that men could fly."

Paid less than servicemen, the women in the WDs, the Women's Royal Canadian Naval Service and Canadian Women's Army Corps occupied traditional roles - and found new ones. CWACs became stenographers, clerks and kitchen workers while WDs worked in 65 of the 103 RCAF trades by 1944. A WD ran the Orderly Room at one base: "I never ran into the feeling that a woman shouldn't be there," while another became an intelligence officer, debriefing bomber crews. WRENS served as signallers and endured the blitz in London.

Wilmer Nadjiwon, an Ojibwa from Cape Croker Reserve in Owen Sound, had a steady job in a brick factory when war broke out. For his friends, joining the Army meant "good pay, a dollar and a half a day." Nadjiwon enlisted on impulse in 1942, and served as an anti-tank gunner in Italy. He remembered being issued with a blanket and told: "Take care of it - because it's the one we'll bury you in."

The 1st Canadian Division arrived in Britain in December and trained at Aldershot during the coldest January since 1894. About half a million Canadian servicemen and women spent some time in Britain during the war. Charlie Hobbs, an air gunner, noted how they resented the class system in Britain. Bored, homesick, baffled by the British fondness for Brussels sprouts, kippers and warm beer, Canadian soldiers drilled and waited for the German invasion that never came.

On May 10, 1940, the Germans unleashed their blitzkrieg (lightning war). Their panzer armies, spearheaded by tanks, swiftly overran Holland, Belgium, Luxembourg and Northern France. Lt. Gen. "Andy" McNaughton refused to commit Canadian troops to a lost cause as the British evacuated their defeated army from Dunkirk between May 27 and June 4. On June 12, however, the 1st Brigade of the 1st Canadian Infantry Division landed at Brest just before Paris fell and the French army disintegrated. The troops reached Sablé-sur-Sarthe, 250 kms southwest of Paris. Then they were ordered to return to Britain.

Two CWACs service a Sherman tank at Longue Point Ordnance Depot, Québec, April 1944. DND

Canadians in trucks and on trains bristling with weapons headed for Brest but ended up in St. Malo. Units destroyed their vehicles and heavy weapons. But Lt. Col. J.H. Roberts, commanding officer of the 1st Field Regiment, Royal Canadian Horse Artillery, refused to abandon his guns, noting: "Although there was evidently no enemy within 200 miles, the withdrawal was conducted like a rout." The RCHA was the only artillery unit under British command to bring its guns back from France.

In June 1940, Canadians garrisoned Iceland. In August 1941, some went to Spitzbergen, north of Norway, to destroy coal mines so that they would not fall into enemy hands. In August 1943, the 13th Canadian Infantry Brigade landed with American troops at Kiska in the Aleutians, only to discover that the Japanese had withdrawn in the previous month. With them went a unique American-Canadian unit, the 1st Special Service Force. Formed in 1942 as an élite body, the "Devil's Brigade" saw heavy action in Italy in 1943-44.

Most Canadian soldiers waited for action in Britain. On Christmas Day, 1942, some of them fought members of the British Black Watch in the streets of Camberley with boots and broken bottles.

Half a world away the British surrendered the colony of Hong Kong to the Japanese on that day, and hundreds of their comrades, the first Canadians to see action, went into a long, brutal captivity.

Canadian soldiers in training in England. NAC

HONG KONG
December 1941

"We knew...there'd be no escape. There was no way it could be defended."

Pvt. George Barron on arrival in Hong Kong.

The members of "C" Force, consisting of a brigade headquarters and two infantry battalions, reached Hong Kong on November 16. On December 8, the day after their attack on Pearl Harbor, the Japanese launched their assault on the British colony. The Canadians joined 12,000 British and Indian troops in a forlorn hope because British generals in London believed that they would have "a very great moral effect in the whole of the Far East."

Ottawa assigned the Royal Rifles of Canada and the Winnipeg Grenadiers under Brigadier John Lawson to help in the defence of Hong Kong. Embarking at Vancouver on HMT *Awatea* and HMCS *Prince Robert*, the troops trained on the ships, suddenly realizing they would be the first ones from the country to go into action. A foul-up sent most of their vehicles to the Philippines.

Leaving their ships, members of "C" Force marched through the city "steel-helmeted and obviously invincible" as one soldier put it. Then the Canadians settled into the comfortable and complacent life of the colony. For 23 cents a week, a servant would do their laundry, shave them and bring them tea in bed.

North of Kowloon, on the mainland, lay the first British defence position, the Gin Drinkers Line. The Canadians took up their posts on the island of Hong Kong. Pvt. Wilf Lynch realized "that if the Japanese attacked they'd wipe us out."

The battle-hardened enemy swarmed over the land defences and launched an amphibious attack on the island on December 18. Major W. A. Bishop of the Rifles requested artillery fire on a fort seized by the Japanese. He was informed that friendly forces held it so went to investigate. Meeting a Japanese patrol, he opened up with his tommy gun. With another officer, he killed seven of the enemy and the others retreated. Bishop received the DSO for this action.

Winnipeg Grenediers entrain for Hong Kong, Oct 25, 1941. NAC

On December 20, the Grenadiers took Mount Butler, a key position, at bayonet point then lost it in a counterattack. CSM John Osborn threw himself on an enemy grenade, saving the lives of seven of his men but losing his own. Osborn's bravery won him a posthumous VC. Brigadier Lawson died fighting outside his headquarters, a pistol in each hand. The Grenadiers denied the enemy the use of the main north-south road across the island for three days until they ran out of food, water and ammunition. On Christmas Day, D Company of the Rifles lost 104 of 148 men attacking a Japanese position near the southern tip of the island.

While Canadian soldiers died in this desperate siege, Prime Minister Mackenzie King sent a message praising their bravery as "an inspiration to us all."

The colony surrendered on Christmas Day. During and after the battle, the Japanese behaved barbarously, killing the wounded and prisoners. Nursing Sisters Kay Christie and May Waters went with the Canadian contingent and tended the wounded at the British Military Hospital on Bowen Road. Under shell and sniper fire, the nurses evacuated patients from the second and third floors and then witnessed Japanese atrocities in the hospital before being interned in Stanley Camp. Here the nurses endured boredom and hunger as "one endless day rolled into another." In September 1943, both were repatriated to Canada.

The soldiers who survived the battle became slave labourers in coal and iron mines in Japan and on airfield construction in Hong Kong. They struggled to survive in unbelievable squalor on a few hundred calories a day. As one Canadian put it: "Our entire identity was removed... There seemed to be no escape, no exit this side of the grave." Paddy Keenan, RSM of the Grenadiers, kept up the spirits of the men: "He moved in an enchanted aura of untouchable certainty... exuding defiant confidence." A soldier who survived the battle and the camps titled his book *Where Life and Death Held Hands*.

The Canadians lost 290 officers and men at Hong Kong, and 287 more in prison camps. The life expectancy of those who survived was reduced by ten to 15 years.

Members of the Royal Rifles of Canada disembark at Hong Kong, November 16, 1942 NAC

The government appointed Chief Justice Lyman Duff of the Supreme Court to head an enquiry into the Hong Kong disaster. The commission largely exonerated the government, but found some senior officers had not acted efficiently. Mackenzie King told the judge that his report "will help to give the people of Canada a confidence in their administration, which means everything to this country's war effort."

But when Canadian soldiers next went into battle, they suffered an even worse defeat - and heavier causalities than at Hong Kong - in the badly planned assault on Dieppe.

Top: The Pacific Star, awarded to those who served in Hong Kong.
Bottom: Some of the survivors of the battle and the Japanese camps after their liberation in August 1945, Shamshuipo Camp, Hong Kong. NAC

This poster celebrates Lt. Col. Merritt's bravery at Dieppe. AMHC

DIEPPE
August 19, 1942

"All in all, it was a very, very poorly planned operation. We were slaughtered…I still can't understand why it was Canadians who were sacrificed at Dieppe."

Pvt. Thomas Hunter, Royal Regiment of Canada.

With 1,945 of his comrades, Hunter became a German prisoner of war. Another 907 died, either at Dieppe or in captivity in the greatest single disaster in Canadian military history.

Why did this happen?

The Americans and the Soviet Union wanted a Second Front in Europe, and Lord Louis Mountbatten, ambitious and inexperienced, sought to test out his ideas on amphibious warfare. Canadian generals and some politicians thought their soldiers should see some action. The plan for the landing, drawn up without Canadian participation, claimed that "Dieppe is lightly defended." Aerial reconnaissance failed to locate German batteries in cliffs overlooking the beaches.

About 6,100 men, 5,000 of them Canadians, took part in "Operation Jubilee." While crossing the English Channel, the invasion armada bumped into a German convoy. As it approached the French coast, enemy guns opened up on it. At 5.20 a.m., 20 minutes behind schedule, the Royals and three platoons of the Black Watch landed at Puys, east of Dieppe. Thomas Hunter recalled "the machine-guns in the pillboxes just raking away, killing everybody as they came off the ships." With another soldier he tried to haul a mortar across the sand. Seeing his companion shot, Hunter found an alcove in a cliff and began firing his rifle at a pillbox. He noted that the Germans "weren't killing too many ordinary soldiers; they were getting the NCOs and the officers." Only 20 Royals reached the top of the cliff where they hid out until they surrendered at 4.20 p.m. Those on the beach did so at 8.30 a.m. Two hundred others died in action.

The beach after the Dieppe raid. NAC

The Royal Hamilton Light Infantry (the Rileys) and the Essex Scottish landed at 5.20 a.m. Clearing strongpoints, they went over the heavily wired seawall and fought in the casino and the streets. Dieppe marked the first use of Churchill tanks in battle. Those of the Calgary Regiment advanced towards the town, tracks spinning in the shingle. A few reached the town and covered the retreating troops. Then these tanks and those immobilized on the beach continued to fire as the Canadians tried to reach the landing craft. No tanks, and only one tank crew, returned from Dieppe.

The South Saskatchewan Regiment landed at Pourville and headed up the valley of the Scie. German fire killed scores of them as they crossed a bridge. Their commander, Lt. Col. Cecil Merritt strode over the bridge, his helmet on his arm, "like he was taking a stroll," and rallied his men. Lt. Col. Gosling, commander of the Queen's Own Cameron Highlanders, landing to support Merritt's men, died as he stepped on to the beach. Merritt fought a rearguard action with a few men before surrendering and received one of the two VCs awarded at Dieppe. The other went to the first Canadian padre to win it.

Capt. J.W. Foote of the Rileys treated wounded on the beach and carried others to landing craft. Opting to stay with his men, he became a prisoner of war.

Acting as a reserve, Les Fusiliers Mont-Royal landed at 7 a.m. and found themselves pinned down on the beach. Two of its members generated smoke, knocked out a pillbox, and manned the 6-pounder gun of an abandoned tank. Then some soldiers raised white flags: "The Germans took our rifles…They were quite easygoing. Everyone felt relief." The enemy lost 121 killed and 212 wounded.

Churchill described Operation Jubilee as "an indispensable preliminary to full-scale operations" that yielded valuable lessons for D-Day.

Dieppe has returned to being a pleasant summer resort.

Memorials to the Canadians who landed here face the beaches where so many died. The nearby cemetery at Hautot-sur-Mer holds 656 dead, including 121 who could not be identified, proof of the savagery of the short, futile battle.

Brigadier Denis Whitaker, then a captain, landed with the Rileys. With his wife, Shelagh, he set out to determine why the attack on Dieppe ended in disaster and concluded: "My hardest lesson… after all my years of careful and sometimes painful research, was in not finding pat answers to everything. Gaps will always remain in the 'how' and 'why.' "

SICILY AND ITALY
1943-45

"In all, 92,757 Canadians served in the Italian theatre and 26,254 were killed or wounded, figures that speak for themselves as to the ferocity of the struggle."

Fred Cederberg, "Postscript", *The Long Road Home.*

On July 5, 1943, HMV *Devis* slowly made its way towards Sicily, carrying vehicles, stores and soldiers. Then a torpedo ripped into the ship. Major Doug Harkness of the Royal Canadian Artillery, commander of the troops on board, organized the orderly evacuation of the men, and rescued those trapped on the mess deck. He received the George Medal for his leadership, later becoming Canada's Minister of National Defence.

Frank O'Donnell, still two months short of his 18th birthday, landed with the 1st Canadian Division near Pachino in Sicily on July 10. His landing craft hit a sandbar and he jumped into neck-deep water. His unit had lost its guns when the *Devis* and two other ships went down "so there was confusion about what we were supposed to be doing."

The Canadians formed part of the British 8th Army, under General Montgomery. The Canadians suffered only seven killed and 23 wounded on their first day in enemy territory - and captured 680 Italians. Then the infantrymen and the tanks of the Three Rivers Regiment from the 1st Canadian Army Tank Brigade set off to seize a series of hill towns held by the enemy. The German defence strategy in Italy involved fighting holding actions at certain points, delaying Allied advances and killing as many of the soldiers as possible, then retreating to carefully prepared positions and standing firm there. General Harry Crerar, a First World War veteran, grumbled: "This war is so much like the last one, it's not even funny." In heat and dust in summer and mud and rain in winter, Canadian troops slogged across Sicily and up the boot of Italy, bedeviled by jaundice, dysentery and malaria as well as fighting a skilled, tenacious enemy.

O'Donnell recalled the awful poverty of the Sicilians and the landscape: "It was all hills - rugged terrain and dry. The roads were powder, so every movement sent up huge clouds of dust." The Canadians fought through 250 km of hill country to reach the Strait of Messina, losing 562 killed, 1,664 wounded and 84 captured. The assault on Assoro illustrates the difficulties of combat in this kind of country. The town stands on a thousand-metre hill. Lt. Col. Bruce Sutcliffe, commanding officer of the Hastings and Prince Edward Regiment (the Hasty Ps) went

out with an intelligence officer, Lt. Battle Cockin, to examine the cliff his men would have to climb to reach Assoro. A German shell killed both of them. Major the Lord Tweedsmuir took command of the regiment, and led his men up a steep cliff overlooking the town - in the dark. As Farley Mowat put it: "…each of us performed his own private miracle. From ledge to ledge we oozed upwards like some vast mould." From the cliff top, they saw Germans going about their daily duties. The Hasty Ps attacked, and called for artillery support as the 48th Highlanders assaulted the town from below.

Crossing the Strait of Messina on September 3, the Allied armies began to move up the Italian peninsula. Then, it seemed, the war in Italy would end.

On July 23, King Victor Emmanuel III, supported by the Italian Army's High command, had dismissed the Italian dictator Mussolini and had him arrested. On September 8, the Italian government announced an armistice with the Allies. On the following day, the Germans rescued Mussolini as their reinforced armies continued to fight. Churchill saw the Italian campaign as an attack on the "soft underbelly" of Europe and as a way of tying down troops that could be used to defend the continent from invasion. It proved to be a tough undertaking.

A German general in Sicily reported of the Canadians: "In fieldcraft superior to our own troops. Very mobile at night, surprise break-ins, clever infiltration at night with small groups between our strongpoints."

Much of Italy, with the spine of the Apennine Mountains running up its centre, seems designed for defence. The Canadians captured Reggio di Calabria against little opposition, took Catanzaro and were 120 km inland a week after landing on the toe of Italy. In deteriorating weather, the troops made their way up the Apennine Mountains. On October 1, they fought the Germans at Motta Montecorvino, taking Campobasso two weeks later. Tanks from the Three Rivers Regiment supported the British assault on Termoli on the Adriatic coast and then advanced across the valley of the Sangro River.

The Germans stood and fought, then moved back up the peninsula. They built strong positions across the waist of the country south of Rome (the Winter, Hitler and Gustav lines) and north of Tuscany (the Gothic Line). They also took advantage of a natural line of defence in front of Ortona, giving Canadians one of the hardest battles of the war.

Between December 1 and 31, 1943, the 1st Canadian Infantry Division suffered 2,339 casualties, including 502 killed. Over 1,600 officers and men were evacuated because of sickness. Pvt. A.K.Harris recalled a friend suffering from battle fatigue being examined by a patient medical officer at a Regimental Aid Post: "There is deep humiliation in my friend's face… He thinks he has let his friends down… He will be back again and again… going to the breaking point.'

Nine Canadian regiments attacked across the Gully south of Ortona and then fought in the city: the Hasty Ps, the Royals, the "Loyal Eddies" (the Loyal Edmonton Regiment), the Princess Pat's, the Seaforth Highlanders of Canada, the West Nova Scotia Regiment, the Van Doos, the Carleton and

York Regiment and the 48th Highlanders. The Germans dug in on the reverse slopes of the Moro River valley and the Gully, safe from direct artillery fire, in what looked like impregnable positions. On December 12, the West Novas attacked dug-in panzer grenadier positions at the Gully. Dozens of machine-guns and German tanks opened up on them. The battalion's war diary reported: "...all we can do is hope to hold until other plans are made."

On December 14, Capt. Paul Triquet of the Van Doos with seven tanks of the Ontario Regiment led 50 men through a mined, muddy valley to attack Casa Berardi, a German strongpoint. In the roar of battle, he shouted: "There are enemy in front of us, behind us and on our flanks. There is only one safe place...our objective." The tanks, under Major Snuffy Smith, and Triquet's men took Casa Berardi and held it against repeated counterattacks. Triquet won the first Canadian VC of the Mediterranean campaign, noting: "My young French Canadians were superb." Smith received the MC. Major Strome Galloway summarized his war in *Bravely Into Battle*. The company commander in the Royals described the attack on Ortona as "a walk into catastrophe." Mortar and machine-gun fire cut down the regiment's strength to 18 officers and 159 men. Galloway wished a grimly smiling Cpl. J.E.Morton luck as the Bren-gunner trudged into a vineyard. This man had lost his brother at Assoro and soon, too, he lay dead.

Tough paratroopers defended Ortona as Canadian troops tried to encircle the city. The Loyal Eddies and the Seaforth Highlanders took Ortona house by house, blowing holes in connecting walls in a process known as "mouseholing." Tanks of the Three Rivers Regiment provided fire support as infantry probed the dangerous, fire-swept streets. The Germans fought skillfully, leaving behind booby-traps. One of Pvt. Smoky Smith's men saw a much-prized German knife sticking out of a jar and reached for it. Smith told him to desist and pushed the jar out of the window with his rifle butt. It hit the street and exploded.

The battle went on through Christmas Day. At Santa Maria di Constantinopoli, the Seaforth Highlanders enjoyed a splendid dinner. The troops rotated through the church as German shells fell nearby. Each company had two hours to enjoy soup, pork with applesauce, cauliflower, vegetables, mashed potatoes, gravy, Christmas pudding and minced pies.

The "weary, strained and dirty" soldiers listened to carols sung by an improvised choir, accompanied on the organ by Lt. Wilf Gildersleeve, a Signals officer. And then they went out to kill and be killed on this holy day. Other troops dined on bully beef, washed down with local wine.

Pvt. Jack Bailey, Perth Regiment, near Orsogna, Jan 1944. NAC

At 11 p.m. on the night of December 27, the Germans began to quit the town. Charles Comfort, the war artist, painted a vivid picture of the devastation: "The Plaza Plebiscita presented another depressing rock pile, the Sherman tank 'Amazing' tilted and brewed up at its centre. We looked about in bewilderment and exhaustion. One felt a choking claustrophobia in the place. Everywhere was misery, death and destruction. I could not possibly paint, or even sketch."

North of Ortona, the Cape Breton Highlanders and the Perth Regiment attacked a ridge overlooking the Arielli Valley on January 17, 1944. The troops went in at 5.30 a.m. across open ground. A gunner reported: "I could see the infantry going ahead of us and being cut down." The attack failed, as did another in the afternoon, and on that day the Cape Bretoners lost 47 killed, 62 wounded and 29 captured. One man with his leg off lay in a ditch for four days until someone saw him signaling with a piece of a mirror and his comrades rescued him. CSM Joe Oldford of the Cape Bretoners recalled that "it was supposed to be... a flanking movement but somewhere along the line someone had changed the plans," and the troops went straight up the centre and were pinned down.

The Italian campaign on the east coast of the country involved crossing numerous rivers overlooked by German troops, who dominated the high ground. Patrols went out, freezing as flares went up, avoiding Schuch mines that sent out showers of ball bearings when they exploded. Alert to every sound, the Canadians reconnoitered enemy positions and sought prisoners. One soldier wrote of "the whistling shells and whirr of bullets...My nerves are not what they used to be and Jerry is really putting up quite a fight." Wounded men and those suffering from battle exhaustion trickled back to Regimental Aid Posts in the rear, to be patched up and evacuated to hospitals. Here, between clean sheets, they were tended to by Canadian nurses and doctors.

During the South African War, the Nursing Service became an integral part of the Canadian Army Medical Corps, with nurses granted the rank, pay and allowances of lieutenants. The first contingent of nurses to serve in the Second

---

Top: War artist Lawren Harris at work near Ortona, in front of a destroyed German tank, in March 1944. DND
Bottom: A Canadian Christmas in Ortona. NAC

World War left Canada for England in June, 1940, to staff two Canadian general hospitals. After the Dieppe raid, one of the hospitals performed 95 operations in 19 1/2 hours. A group of "grimy, tin–hatted girls, perspiring in the terrific heat and burdened with cumbersome equipment" arrived in Sicily after the Allied invasion. These nurses, and others who came later, served in five hospitals in Italy and with two major mobile medical units of the 1st Canadian Corps as it moved up the peninsula. Early in 1944, No.4 Field Surgical Unit first used penicillin, then a new wonder drug, to treat a fractured femur. This unit was also the first to have a nursing sister in its operating theatre in a forward area. One nursing sister with a field unit wrote: "To me personally, it was the most challenging, inspiring and soul-satisfying work I have ever done."

By the end of the war, the Royal Canadian Army Medical Corps had 3,656 nursing sisters on its strength, two-thirds of them serving overseas. Nursing sisters also served with the RCAF and RCN, and all carried away with them memories of patients who survived and those who died. Alexandra Bury recalled soldiers in No. 10 General Hospital in Normandy as "polite and easy to look after. They endured their injuries bravely and I remember many of them fondly and sadly." Marion Crawford tried to treat the chest wound of a "husky

While some Canadian soldiers advance on foot, others make use of local transport in Italy. NAC

young fellow" from the Queen's Own - but he died. A 17-year-old patient named Struthers seemed to be doing well after his operation: "One afternoon, he suddenly died... The memory of that young soldier is still with me after forty-seven years."

As the casualties mounted in Italy, fewer and fewer reinforcements reached the front lines. And they lacked training. An officer recalled seeing a newly arrived lieutenant being briefed before an attack near Ortona. A day later he noticed the man's body under a blanket.

In April and May 1944, the 8th Army moved in secret across Italy to assist the American Fifth Army in its drive to Rome. Canadians in the "Devil's Brigade" had already seen action here. An assault battalion led by Lt. Col. Tommy MacWilliam climbed Monte di Difensa, a strong German redoubt leading to Cassino, in two nights. Sgt. Ken Cashman noted: "I honestly don't know how some of us did it." A mule broke down, and one of the Canadians took its load and carried it the rest of the way. The Canadians took the Germans by surprise and captured the position in an hour. As Cashman put it: "It was still more like a training exercise, until we got to the top and discovered it wasn't a training exercise...It scared the hell out of me." The Special Force then spent six hard days in battle, taking 511 casualties including 73 dead and 116 exhaustion cases. MacWilliam died in a mortar blast.

Major Bill Pell of the Carleton and York Regiment remembers the attack on the Hitler Line as his worst battle. His men confronted rolls of barbed wire and German guns with interlocking fields of fire. He watched four British tanks crush the barbed wire in front of his position: "They all brewed up - only one man escaped." On May 23, Pell took 40 of his men through the wire and breached the Hitler Line. On the following day, Lt. E.J. Perkins of the Strathconas established a bridgehead over the Melfa River beyond the Line. While his light tanks held off the enemy, Major J.K. Mahony of the Westminsters led his men over to join him. Wounded in the head and leg, he kept fighting, exhorting his men to hold the position and received the VC. Perkins won the DSO, a rare award for a junior officer.

Rome, declared an open city, fell on June 4, as the Special Service Force moved in at 6.20 in the morning and seized key locations. Lt. Col. Tom Gilday, a Canadian, noted: "The city was dead. Nobody dared stick their noses out...they didn't know which flag to put out or whether to cheer or cry."

After the fall of Rome, the Canadians returned to the eastern side of the Apennines and experienced some of the bitterest fighting of the campaign. To reach Rimini, their objective, they had to pierce the Gothic Line, the last major German

A familiar winter scene in "sunny Italy." NAC

Canadian tanks advancing between the Gustav and Hitler Lines, Liri Valley, 24 May, 1944. DND

defence - and cross six rivers. On August 25, four battalions of the 1st Canadian Infantry Division crossed the Matauro River as artillery opened up on German positions. They found the enemy front lines empty and moved over broken ground to the Foglia River where soldiers died in mine-thick flats. On August 30, the Cape Breton Highlanders and the Perth Regiment moved across the river to attack Monteluro, which overlooked the town of Montecchio. Joe Oldford led a daylight assault against Germans on high ground as they plastered his men with accurate fire. Oldford re-organized the scattered soldiers in the forward positions and they held the line for five hours. He received the DCM, but did not tell his family about it until 40 years later. On September 10, the Carleton and York Regiment pushed forward across a deep gully eight kms south-west of Rimini under intense shell and mortar fire, opening a bridgehead for the 8th Army.

The Royals attacked an airfield near Rimini. Here Strome Galloway found the body of a German paratrooper. His pockets contained death notices for three of his brothers and snapshots of a happy family in the hometown of Zweibrucken. Two hundred years earlier, the ancestors of the officer's mother had moved from the town to Canada. He wrote that he "never was a German hater" and that few fighting men were.

Canadian troops entered the deserted city of Rimini on September 21. Then the rains came, rivers flooded, and tanks bogged down in the swampy lands of the Romagna.

And the Germans kept resisting the Allied advance.

On the night of October 21, the Princess Pat's established a bridgehead across the Savio River and the Loyal Eddies and the Seaforths joined them. The Germans attacked with three Panther tanks, two self-propelled guns, and 30 infantry. Torrential rain raised the river level two metres in five hours, preventing Canadian tanks and guns from moving forward to support the embattled infantry. Pvt. Smoky Smith picked up a PIAT (Projector, Infantry, Anti-Tank), a weapon not known for accuracy or reliability. Standing a few metres in front of an advancing tank, he knocked it out. Picking up his tommy gun, he killed four German soldiers and drove the rest back. Smith held his position, protecting a wounded comrade, until the attack ended, winning the third and final Canadian VC of the Italian campaign.

After months of fighting, the front bogged down and stabilized with the Allies unable to break into the Lombardy Plain. The Italian campaign continued into the spring of 1945. But by then the soldiers of the 1st Canadian Corps had joined their comrades in Northwest Europe.

Fred Cederberg recorded his experiences with the Cape Breton Highlanders in *The*

Major John Mahony, VC and Lt. "Perky" Perkins, DSO

Long Road Home. It presents a view of the Italian campaign from the slit trench. In his first action, British troops fired on the assault companies, mistaking them for Germans. And their commander told them: "Nobody stops for men who've been hit. No attack can succeed unless you keep moving." Mortar shells fell on a group of soldiers, tearing the arm off one man. He died before a stretcher-bearer reached him. The soldiers became numbed. After a shell obliterated another man, they did not mourn: "He was a stranger. They hardly knew him."

After being ambushed, an enemy officer raised a white flag and asked permission to recover his dead and wounded. Cederberg gave it – and lent the Germans stretchers and morphine. They were later returned – with a bottle of schnapps. The diarist of the 1st Division recorded that on December 25: "Greetings were exchanged across the short no man's land but this time not with bullets." A German soldier displayed a white flag on the bank of the Senio River then shouted to the Canadians: "Why don't you surrender?"

Replacements came to Cederberg's unit, and he advised one to dig a deep slit trench. The man ignored this good advice, and after a shelling they found his body – cut in half.

Italy has become prosperous since the war. Poplars shade the roads in Romagna and the fields over which Canadians fought so valiantly doze in the sun. Cars and tour busses easily cross the many rivers where so many bitter actions took place. And 5,799 Canadians who never saw their country again lie in beautifully tended cemeteries. There is no bitterness among the residents of this land about the strangers who came from a far land to fight and suffer in "sunny Italy."

In September 1997, 80 Canadian veterans attended the dedication of a monument on the site of the Gothic Line. Paid for by local townspeople, it overlooks the Po Valley. Victor Cameron of the Hasty Ps was surprised at this gesture by the people over whose land he and his comrades fought: "I guess we were not perceived as conquerors."

The Canadian troops who fought in Italy received the name of "D-Day Dodgers" after the Second Front opened. The designation, attributed to Lady Nancy Astor, rankled. Then someone wrote a song with the title. Apparently, Lady Astor assumed it was a humorous nickname. As Victor Cameron put it: "It doesn't matter any more. We're here and she's not."

Sherman tank at Melfa River.

D-DAY TO V-E DAY
June 6, 1944 – May 7, 1945

"The average Canadian soldier is reasonable, sensible and has the independence and initiative to become difficult if he considers he is being treated unreasonably."

Major R.A. Gregory, neuro-psychiatrist, 3 Canadian Infantry Division, October 1944.

"Robbie" Robinson served in both world wars, surviving the battles of St. Eloi, Vimy and Passchendaele and then landing with the West Novas in Sicily in 1943. As he put it: "In the first one, you had to drive a man. In the second, you had to ask him to do something."

Saving Private Ryan graphically portrayed the American landing at Omaha Beach on June 6, 1944. Canadian troops came ashore to the east, on Juno Beach; here houses facing the beach had been turned into strong points by the Germans. They suffered fewer casualties than the Americans, but showed equal bravery under officers who sought to avoid the frontal attacks that had caused so many casualties in the First World War. As the Canadians settled into landing craft before the assault on Normandy, an officer noted,

"The tension coiled inside everyone like an electrical charge waiting to explode." Troops became seasick as the vessels pitched and tossed in open water. As Cpl. Hughie Rocks of the Queen's Own put it: "I don't care if there are 50 million Germans on the beach; just let me off this goddam boat." The 14,000 members of the 3 Canadian Division had been assigned to two sectors flanking the River Suelles, at Courselles-sur-Mer, Bernières–sur–mer and St. Aubin–sur–Mer. Machine guns raked the attacking troops. While waiting for artillery and the tanks of the 2nd Armoured Brigade to arrive, they engaged in the "3Ds" – Digging, Ducking and Dodging.

Rolph Jackson's 10-man section of A Company of the Queen's Own left the landing craft first: "We were slaughtered.

77

Chaplain H/Capt R.L. Seaborn offers prayers with Royal Engineers before embarking for the D-Day invasion. NAC

Our Support Craft was knocked out so we had no heavy weapons…the sea was red." By the end of D-Day, seven of Jackson's companions lay dead and two had been wounded. B Company landed at Bernières, right in front of a strongpoint they planned to outflank, taking heavy casualties before destroying it.

A gunner recalled how things went awry with the Royal Canadian Artillery as it tried to land its guns: " What action goes to plan?" His craft circled for hours and then the troop landed and sought the Royal Winnipeg Rifles (the "Pegs"). A captain wanted a house taken out. The gunners unlimbered their weapon and fired. They had forgotten to remove the muzzle cover and to clean grease off the barrel and the breech. The cover went sailing down the road and the gun stood enveloped in smoke: "When the smoke cleared the gun sat alone and the crew had taken cover in a ditch."

Moving off the beaches, the Canadians advanced on German positions, passing a café 100 metres from the beach selling wine. They made good progress. In mid-afternoon Canadian armour cut the Caen-Bayeux Road after advancing 16 km, the furthest penetration inland made by the Allies on D-Day. The success of the Canadians came at a cost of just under a thousand casualties, including 335 dead.

Then the Battle for Normandy began. Canadians faced the fanatical troops of the 12th SS Panzer Division. They included experienced officers and NCOs who had served in Russia and unblooded former

Canadian tanks come ashore on the afternoon of June 6, 1944. NAC

JUNO BEACH D DAY

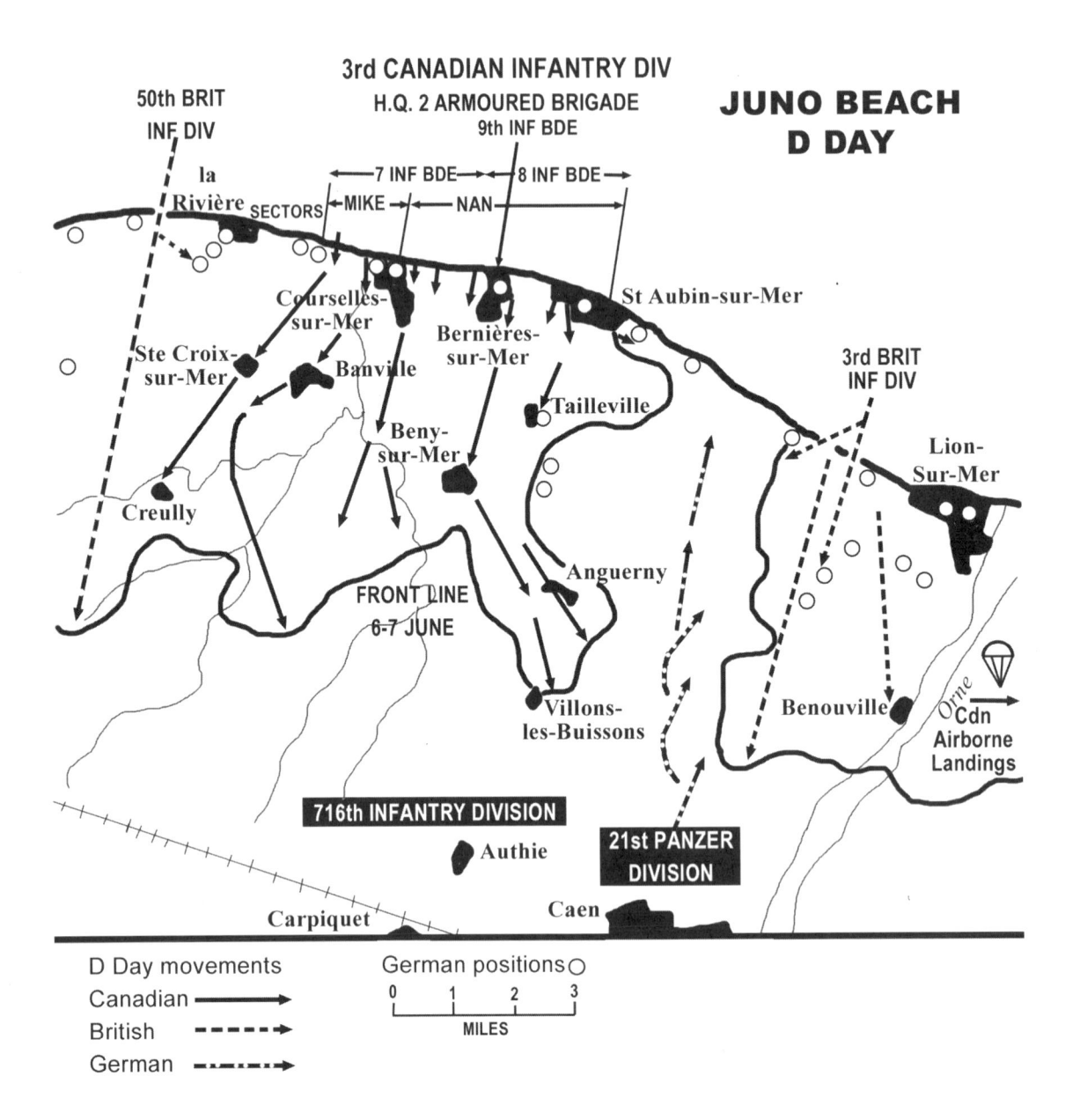

3rd CANADIAN INFANTRY DIV
H.Q. 2 ARMOURED BRIGADE
9th INF BDE
← 7 INF BDE → ← 8 INF BDE →
← MIKE → ← NAN →

50th BRIT INF DIV

la Rivière — SECTORS

Courselles-sur-Mer
Ste Croix-sur-Mer
Banville
Bernières-sur-Mer
Tailleville
St Aubin-sur-Mer

3rd BRIT INF DIV

Creully
Beny-sur-Mer
Anguerny
Lion-Sur-Mer

FRONT LINE 6-7 JUNE

Villons-les-Buissons
Benouville
Orne
Cdn Airborne Landings

716th INFANTRY DIVISION
Authie

21st PANZER DIVISION

Carpiquet   Caen

D Day movements
Canadian ——→
British -- -- →
German —·—·→

German positions ○

0 1 2 3
MILES

members of the Hitler Youth. On the morning of June 7, they counterattacked, captured Canadian soldiers and shot 23 of them at Buron, a village northwest of Caen. Members of the 12th SS continued this practice throughout the Normandy campaign, and as one account put it: "There was certainly retaliation for these atrocities."

Le Régiment de la Chaudière took the town of Beny-sur-Mer in the late afternoon of June 6. The Canadians had learned the lesson of Dieppe and HMCS *Algonquin* knocked out a battery of German 88 mm guns blocking their advance. Members of the 1st Canadian Parachute Battalion, dropped behind the bridgehead, seized a German headquarters and destroyed two bridges over the Dives and Divette Rivers. After taking heavy casualties, they seized the strategic crossroads at Le Mesnil. The North Novas, aided by tanks of the Sherbrooke Fusiliers, took the village of Buron. Then they moved ahead of their artillery support in nearby Authie. The Sherman tanks proved no match for the German Panthers and many fell to their guns.

The 3rd Division held its lines, suffering 3,000 casualties, about a third of them killed, in six days of fighting. By June 12, the Allied bridgehead formed one continuous front 97 kms long and 24 kms deep. The North Shore (New Brunswick) Regiment and the Pegs suffered heavy casualties in the assault on Carpiquet air base in early July; the nearby wheat fields were strewn with their dead. The Allies had hoped to capture Caen on D-Day. Before the Canadians advanced to take it, the RAF bombed the city into rubble on July 8. Canadians entered Caen on the following day to find that the Germans had withdrawn to its outskirts before the bombs fell.

Canadian infantry learned warfare the hard way as the Germans defended key positions to block their advance. Verrières Ridge dominates a road leading south from Caen. The Black Watch of Canada made two attempts to capture it, losing 307 of the 325 members who went into battle.

After Caen fell, the Americans began a pincer movement to encircle the German troops in Normandy, with the Canadians driving south towards Falaise on August 7 to link up with them. Operation Totalize involved another example of Canadian creativity, the invention of the Armoured Personnel Carrier (APC) to take troops into battle. This concept resulted in the creation of the 1st Canadian Armoured Carrier Regiment. Totalize started badly. American bombers dropped short, killing and wounding Canadian and Polish

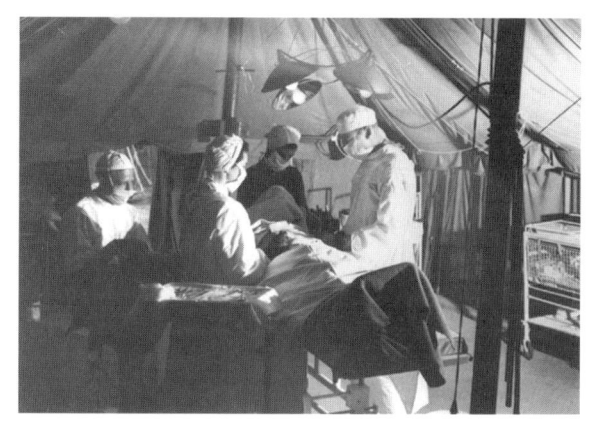

Top: An operation at No 8 Canadian General Hospital, Bayeux, France, August 1944. DND
Bottom: Canadian tankers take time out to warm themselves. AMHC

Canadian soldiers rush through a contested town. NAC
At top: The France and Germany Star, awarded for service in those countries and in Belgium and Holland between June 6, 1944 and May 8, 1945.

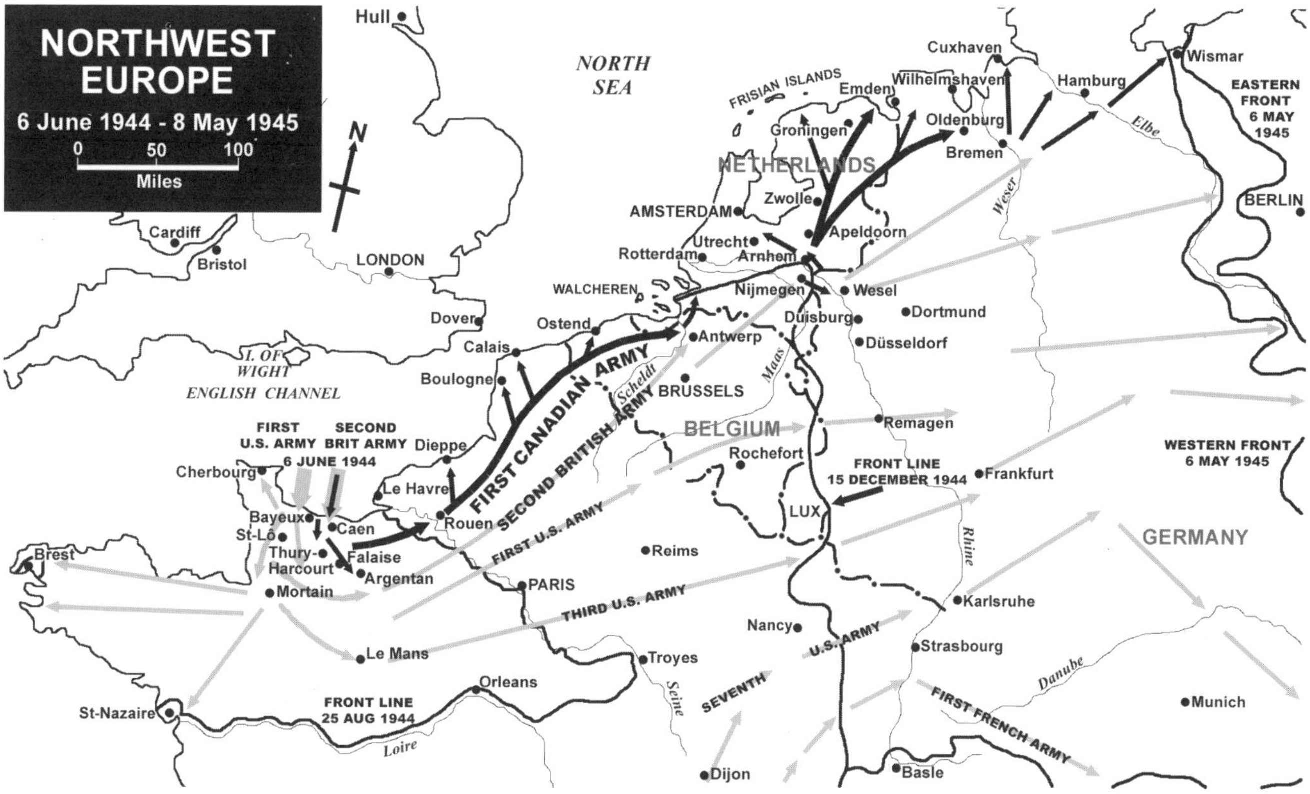
NORTHWEST EUROPE
6 June 1944 - 8 May 1945
0 50 100
Miles
N
Hull
NORTH SEA
FRISIAN ISLANDS
Emden
Wilhelmshaven
Cuxhaven
Wismar
Hamburg
EASTERN FRONT 6 MAY 1945
Groningen
Oldenburg
Bremen
Elbe
NETHERLANDS
Weser
BERLIN
AMSTERDAM
Zwolle
Apeldoorn
Cardiff
Bristol
LONDON
Utrecht
Rotterdam
Arnhem
WALCHEREN
Nijmegen
Wesel
Dover
Ostend
Duisburg
Dortmund
Calais
Antwerp
Düsseldorf
I. OF WIGHT
ENGLISH CHANNEL
Boulogne
FIRST CANADIAN ARMY
Scheldt
BRUSSELS
Maas
BELGIUM
Remagen
FIRST U.S. ARMY
SECOND BRIT ARMY
6 JUNE 1944
Dieppe
SECOND BRITISH ARMY
Rochefort
WESTERN FRONT 6 MAY 1945
Cherbourg
Le Havre
FRONT LINE 15 DECEMBER 1944
Frankfurt
Bayeux
Caen
Rouen
LUX
St-Lô
Thury-Harcourt
Falaise
Argentan
FIRST U.S. ARMY
Reims
Rhine
GERMANY
Brest
Mortain
PARIS
THIRD U.S. ARMY
Karlsruhe
Nancy
Le Mans
Troyes
SEVENTH U.S. ARMY
Strasbourg
Danube
Orleans
Seine
FIRST FRENCH ARMY
Munich
St-Nazaire
FRONT LINE 25 AUG 1944
Loire
Dijon
Basle

Members of the 1 Canadian Parachute Battalion prepare for D-Day. NAC

soldiers. Then 12th Panzer stopped their advance. The operation, cancelled on August 12, was replaced by Operation Tractable. This time, RAF bombers dumped their loads on Canadian troops racing south to meet American soldiers driving north.

The German soldiers trapped in "The Cauldron" were strafed and bombed by Spitfires and Typhoons, some flown by Canadian pilots, who recalled the smell of death reaching their cockpits. The last road leading out of this killing ground passed through St. Lambert-sur-Dives. A squadron of the South Alberta Regiment, led by Major David Currie, and a company of the Argyll and Sutherland Highlanders blocked the German retreat here, destroying their tanks, guns and vehicles and taking over 2,000 prisoners. Currie won the VC for the feat. As one of his NCOs put it: "We knew at one stage it was going to be a fight to the finish, but he was so cool about it, it was impossible for us to get excited." By August 25, the total of Germans killed, wounded and captured came to 410,000 for the Battle of Normandy. Only 300 members of 12th Panzer, including their commander, Kurt Meyer, escaped. Meyer was tried after the war for the murder of Canadian soldiers and sentenced to death. But this was commuted to life imprisonment and Meyer was released in 1954.

Tractable opened the road to Paris.

The French ports of Dieppe, Boulogne, Calais and Dunkirk had been bypassed as the Allied armies rolled east to take Paris. 1st Canadian Army received the task of taking them and the Channel coast up to Bruges in Belgium, a distance of 350 kms. The Germans fought hard in some places but abandoned other towns. North of the Seine, Sgt. Ross Bell of the 12th Manitoba Dragoons probed ahead of the advance in a Staghound armoured car. Narrowly avoiding an ambush, the vehicle smashed into a German column hauling three anti-tank guns, demolishing it. A Tiger tank failed to recognize the Staghound and then Bell and his men went into action again as they encountered another mass of retreating Germans. They accounted for 300 enemy dead and wounded, 70 to 80 horses and several anti-tank guns. As the regiment's war diary put it: "...they had proved once more that in war, what is seen as luck goes most often to him who is skilled and bold enough to seize the fleeting chance."

On September 1, the 2nd Division

Top: Major David Currie (left, holding pistol) accepts the surrender of German troops at St.-Lambert-Sur-Dives, August 19, 1944. For defending the village against Germans retreating from the Falaise pocket, Currie won the VC. This photo, the only one of its kind, records this achievement. NAC
Bottom: SS General "Panzer" Meyer, charged with war crimes, handcuffed to Maj Arthur Russell with two members of the Royal Winnipeg Rifles, Aurich, Germany, November 12, 1945. DND

Canadian Artillery in Falaise, August 1944. NAC

A Canadian soldier on patrol in France aims his Sten gun. NAC

entered Dieppe without opposition and paraded in honour of those who had taken part in the futile assault on the town two years earlier.

The Germans decided to make a stand at Boulogne. RAF bombers targeted enemy strongpoints, engineers cleared mines, and bulldozers, flame-thrower tanks and assault vehicles moved cautiously into the burning city. Patrols probed unfamiliar streets and alleys as murderous fire cut down those attacking fortified places on the outskirts of the city.

The Stormont, Dundas, and Glengarry Highlanders beat off enemy tank hunters and then had a stroke of luck. A French patriot showed Major Stothart, the only unwounded officer in D Company, a secret tunnel leading into the heart of the Citadel. As its gates were blown and Churchill tanks raked the ramparts, Canadians appeared inside the walls and the enemy surrendered. After six days of hard fighting, the Germans capitulated on September 22.

None of the ports captured by the Canadians had the capacity to handle the enormous quantities of supplies required to keep the Allied armies moving.

Antwerp, in Belgium, fell on September 4, with its 40 km of docks largely intact. But the Germans held the approaches to the port, determined to deny its use to their enemy. And so Canadian, British and Polish troops began the Battle of the Scheldt while

The fog of war, somewhere in Europe.

Troops of 2 Canadian Division march through Dieppe in September 1944, in honour of those who fought there on August 19, 1942. NAC

the rest of Montgomery's soldiers advanced towards Germany. In his memoirs, the British field marshal stated that he had hoped the Canadian Army could take the approaches to Antwerp "while we going for the Ruhr. I was wrong."

By destroying the dykes, the Germans turned the land between Antwerp and the North Sea into a vast, waterlogged morass. Causeways bisected the flooded land, and the Germans commanded the approaches to them. Many Canadian soldiers had died or been wounded in action during the "bloody victory" in Normandy, and poorly trained reinforcements took their place. An intelligence officer reported: "Against tough, seasoned enemy paratroopers [they] were more of a liability than an asset." A medical officer estimated that 15% of the casualties in the Battle of the Scheldt suffered from neuro-psychiatric conditions after three months in combat.

In wet, cold, windy weather, the Canadians captured Woensdrecht on October 16-21. This opened a way for a thrust along the causeway leading to Walcheren Island. The RAF bombed the dykes around the island. The Canadians attacked by land while other troops mounted a water borne invasion and the Germans surrendered. The Canadians advanced across the Leopold Canal and cleared the Germans from the Breskens area south of Walcheren. The channel to Antwerp opened and an Allied convoy sailed into the port on November 28, led by the Canadian-built *Fort Cataraqui*. No one bothered to invite a representative of the Canadian Army to the welcoming ceremony. Between October 1 and November 8, it lost 355 officers and 6,012 men.

The heavy losses in the Italian and European campaigns led to a conscription crisis in Canada. Under the National Resources Mobilization Act, passed in 1940, the government recruited men for home defence. On November 22, 1944, Prime Minister Mackenzie King announced that these men would now be liable for overseas service. About 16,000 of them left Canada – some went to Kiska in the Aleutians – and 69 died.

In February 1945, 1st Canadian Army, the largest ever commanded by a Canadian general, took part in Operation Veritable to destroy the remaining German formations west of the Rhine. Between the Allies and river lay three strong defensive positions – a screen of strong outposts along the western edge of the Reichswald, the Siegfried Line running through it, and the fortified Hochwald area.

Members of the Régiment de Hull wait to embark for Kiska, August 1943. DND

Buffalo amphibious vehicles carry troops across the Scheldt to Hoofdplaat Terneuzen, Belgium, October 13, 1944. NAC

Appeals for Victory Bonds featured maps and individual soldiers.
The Canadians made first contact with the Russians, but did not enter Berlin.

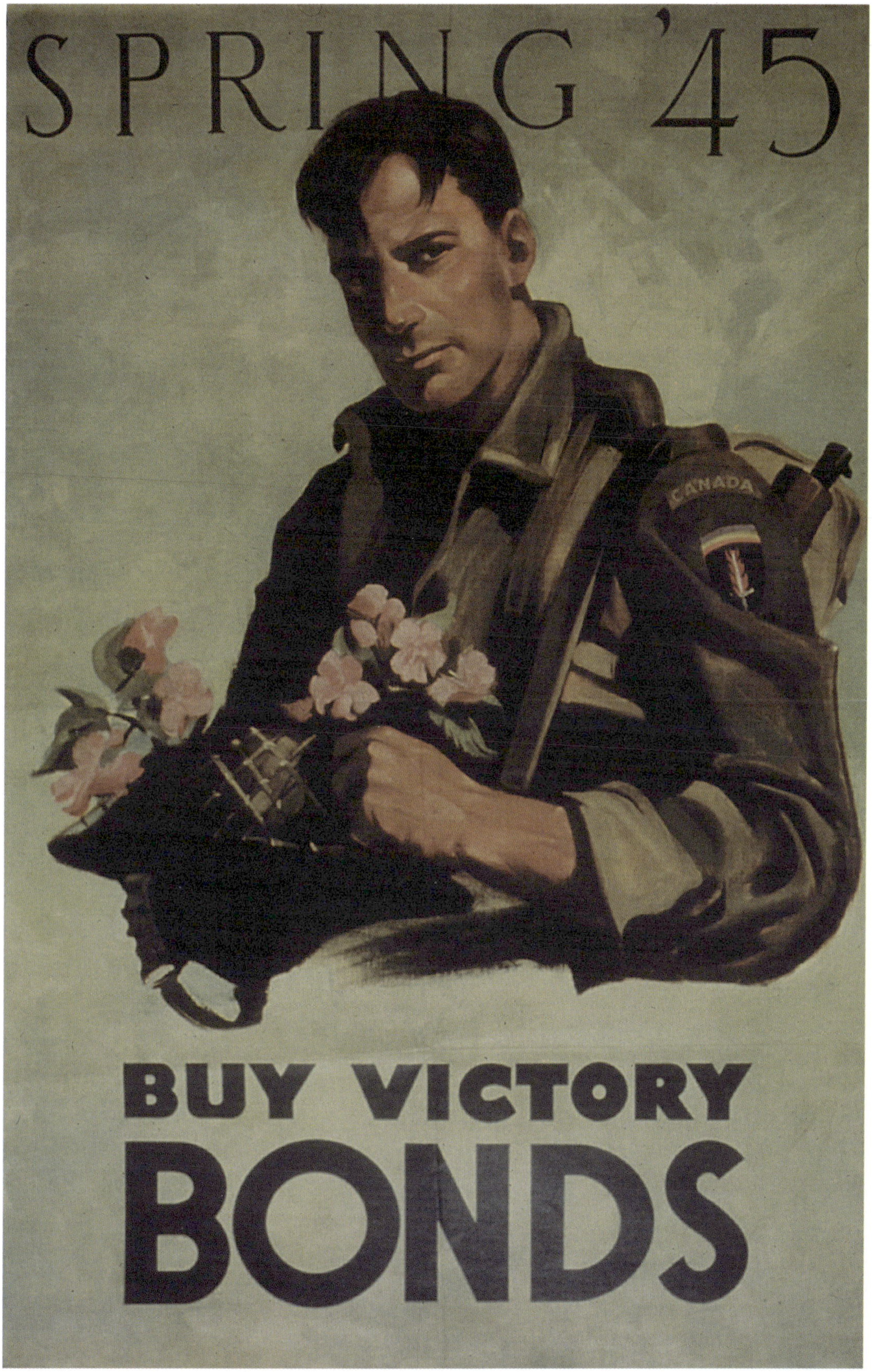
SPRING '45
CANADA
BUY VICTORY
BONDS

The operation began on February 8, 1945, with a thunderous barrage. The Canadians now had plenty of armour and troop carriers, including Wasp flame throwers, Priests (self-propelled guns), and "unfrocked" Priests, vehicles stripped of their guns to carry troops which became known as Kangaroos. They advanced between the Maas and Rhine Rivers over land flooded by the German defenders. On February 19, 68 members of the Canadian Scottish moved towards Moyland Wood, between Cleve and Calcar. The enemy let them approach, then opened fire. Only about 10 Canadian soldiers avoided death or capture. On the night of the same day, Panzer grenadiers counterattacked the 4th Brigade as its troops and tanks struggled along the Goch-Calcar Road, overrunning a position held by the Rileys. Lt. Col. Whitaker, their commander, had prepared for this. His men threw back the enemy who lost many men and seven tanks: Whitaker received the DSO for his leadership.

Shortly after, the Royal Winnipeg Fusiliers, preceded by an artillery barrage and Typhoons that shot up enemy positions, and supported by tanks and Wasps, took Moyland Wood.

The Germans, fighting in their homeland, used dummy artillery to draw fire. Canadian tanks bogged down or went up in flames as the advance moved through the soggy terrain. On the night of 25-26 February, the Queen's Own Rifles set out to capture the hamlet of Mooshof to secure high ground. Sgt. Cosens took his platoon and two tanks towards three farm buildings held by the enemy. Beaten back twice, Cosens ran across open ground to a tank and directed its fire from the turret. Then he attacked the enemy positions with the four survivors of his platoon with the support of the tank. Cosens cleared the buildings only to be killed by a sniper as he set out to report to his company commander. He received a posthumous VC.

Ben Dunkleman, a mortar platoon commander with the Queen's Own, landed on D-Day and took part in the capture of Boulogne. Like other front line soldiers, he often saw surrealistic scenes. At Boulogne, a corporal wearing a silk hat played *The Skater's Waltz* on a "liberated" violin as he led out a string of prisoners. As Dunkleman put it: "Perhaps we were all temporarily insane." Deep in the Reichswald he awoke at 3:30 one morning, wondering if he would ever see the beginning of another day. After one attack, he counted only 36 fighting men left in his company of 115. When a tank commander refused to lead infantry across a forested area sown with mines, Dunkleman threatened to shoot him. It did no good, so the officer called

General Georges Vanier speaks with a wounded black soldier in England. NAC

his men together and asked them if they had any ideas on how to advance without being blown up. Someone suggested that no one would lay mines near trees. So the soldiers hopped from tree to tree through the forest, and Dunkleman later received the DSO for his performance in battle.

Major F.A. Tilston of the Essex Scottish won a VC near Udem. Without tank support, he took his men through a belt of barbed wire, silenced a machine-gun and then fell wounded in the hip. Struggling to his feet, Tilston led his men in vicious hand-to-hand fighting in an elaborate German trench system, until his company was reduced to 26 men. Then the Germans counterattacked and the officer crossed bullet-swept ground again and again to bring grenades and ammunition to his beleagured men. Tilston survived, but both his legs had to be amputated below the knee. Nine days after this action on March 1, German resistance west of the Rhine ended. The Canadian casualties totalled 5,304.

Now the Canadian Corps from Italy joined Canadian Army and the last phase of the war began. On March 23, Canadian soldiers crossed the Rhine in Operation Plunder and advanced west into the Netherlands and north into Germany. On March 24, Cpl. Fred Topham dropped with the 1st Canadian Parachute Battalion on to a heavily defended area east of the Rhine. The medical orderly began to take care of the wounded, then heard a cry for help and watched two of his comrades die as they sought to succour a casualty. Topham went out under fire, gave first aid and then carried the man to shelter. Refusing orders to be evacuated after being wounded, the corporal came across a blazing vehicle. Under fire and with ammunition exploding around him, he rescued its three occupants and received the VC for his bravery, the last to be awarded to a Canadian in the European Theatre.

Canadian troops entered Arnhem and Appledoorn to a rapturous reception from the Dutch. They had suffered through the "Hunger Winter", eating bulbs and anything remotely edible until an arrangement with the German occupiers brought Allied food convoys and air drops.

The Dutch remain forever grateful to their Canadian liberators, teaching their children about the sacrifices these men from another country made to ensure their freedom. In *Thank You Canada*, a Dutch woman recalled seeing six soldiers standing outside her house: They had been in combat for 40 hours without a break. They smiled at being called "Tommies", explaining that they were Canadians and the woman invited them

Every province in Canada told of its contribution to the war effort.

into her home. They shared their rations and took the children to the cookhouse to be fed. The Dutch family felt completely at ease with the Canadian soldiers, noting that: "All of them were afraid." After a pleasant break from battle, the six soldiers left. A sniper killed one of them, and a shell wounded three others. One of the six went to the aid of his friends under fire. He later spent several weeks in hospital with a nervous rash, telling his Dutch hosts: "Well, I guess I'm no hero."

A trooper in the 14th Canadian Hussars wrote home about liberating Germans barges full of wine, food and candy: "…we could get anything we wanted with the candy." Deventer, Zwolle, Groningen, Emden, Wilhelmshaven and Oldenburg fell to the Canadians. All of the Netherlands had now been liberated and troops spread across the North German Plain. Members of the 1st Canadian Parachute Battalion reached Wismar, becoming the first western unit to make contact with the advancing Russians on German soil.

Hitler married his mistress, Eva Braun, on April 29. Both committed suicide on the following day while the Germans fought on. On May 4, 1945, General Harry Crerar, the Canadian commander, ordered his troops to cease attacking the defeated enemy. On that day, Capt. A.E. McCreary, Protestant chaplain of the Grenadier Guards and Lt. N.A. Goldie left their lines to care for German wounded and both were killed. These two brave men were among the last Canadian soldiers to die in the Second World War, on the same day surrender negotiations began. A German staff officer asked Brigadier J.A. Roberts if he was a professional soldier. The Canadian replied: "No, I wasn't a regular soldier. Very few Canadians were. In civilian life I made ice cream."

From D-Day to V-E Day, May 7, Canadians suffered almost 48,000 casualties, about a quarter of whom died in battle or from wounds. Major David Currie, VC, survived the war and just before he died on June 25, 1986, he noted that most people did not know about his award:"Why should they? It's a long time since the war." Major George Hees of the Calgary Highlanders, wounded in the Battle of the Scheldt, later became a popular and effective Minister of Veterans' Affairs. He returned to the Netherlands in May 1985, for a celebration honouring the soldiers who liberated the country. He found the welcome by the Dutch "almost embarassing. We just did our job."

Top: *The Globe and Mail* front page, May 8, 1945. The man portrayed, Wolfgang Nottelman, never went overseas but served as an RCAF test pilot in Churchill, Manitoba. He died on September 30, 2000.
Bottom: Wartime trivia – propaganda appeared everywhere during the war.

IN THE AIR

*"Oh, I have slipped the surly bonds of earth
And danced the skies on laughter-silvered wings;"*

John Gillespie Magee Jr. "High Flight"

Magee, an American serving with the Royal Canadian Air Force (RCAF) wrote his sonnet after first flying a Spitfire. It helped to establish an image of wartime pilots as free spirits soaring into the heavens. The reality of the air war was very different. Magee died in a collision three months after writing his poem.

Canadian pilots excelled in aerial combat in the First World War, and inspired a new generation of flyers in the Second.

But the two conflicts offered radically different challenges for those who flew.

In the spring of 1941, 17-year-old Murray Peden attended a recruiting rally in his home town of Winnipeg. His youthful idol, Billy Bishop, addressed those present, exhilarating Peden and his classmate Ron Dunphy. The two men vowed to join the RCAF as soon as they turned 18, and become pilots. Both served in Bomber Command. Peden achieved his ambition, Dunphy became an observer. The former survived 30 missions, and wrote *A Thousand Shall Fall*, an excellent account of what it meant to be on the front lines of the bomber offensive against Germany. Peden writes of the tensions he and others endured, the small joys, and the death of friends, including Ron Dunphy, who failed to return from a mission to Frankfurt on December 20-21, 1943.

As one airman put it: "The Germans were out to kill us by every possible means." And the RCAF usually received new planes and equipment last. In Bomber Command, aircrew had a one in three chance of survival.

A recruiting poster for the RCAF promises adventure.

Jim Lovelace, also addressed by Billy Bishop, did not know who he was. But he had long been hooked on flying. At the age of five, he screamed and jumped with excitement when he saw his first plane. Lovelace passed his medical for the RCAF on June 17, 1940, and became a Wireless Operator/Air Gunner (WOP/AG). He survived the war and wrote of his experiences in the light-hearted book, *The Flip Side of the Air War*.

Canada began the war with 210 planes, only 37 of them suited to combat. By 1945, the country had the fourth largest Allied air force: during the six years of war, 250,000 men and women wore Air Force blue. Over half the graduates of the British Commonwealth Air Training Plan came from Canada. This programme, carried out at stations across Canada, turned out 131,553 pilots, navigators, air gunners, bomb aimers and other aircrew.

Canadians flew in every kind of aircraft from Lysanders taking British agents in and out of occupied Europe to huge Sunderland flying boats that sought U-boats in the North Atlantic. Canadians defended Malta, flew in the Western Desert of North Africa, participated in the Dam Buster raids, escorted convoys, sowed mines in enemy waters, shot up shipping off Norway, flew cover for troops at Dunkirk and Dieppe, attacked

Wings Presentation, Course No 22, British Commonwealth Air Training Plan, Camp Borden, ON, May 16, 1941. NAC

retreating columns after the D-Day invasion, took aerial photographs, towed gliders to Arnhem and across the Rhine, and engaged in other activities.

Recruits doffed their civilian clothes, put on the uniform of an AC2 (Aircraftsman Second Class) and learned to tell their left foot from their right through endless hours of square bashing. Those selected for air crew wore white flannelette tabs in the front of their wedge caps while in training. Their instructors graded them as pilots, navigators or WOP/AGs. Specialized training followed, and those who passed the courses received their wings. After a period in an ATU (Advanced Training Unit), airmen honed their skills at an OTU (Operational Training Unit). Here pilots "crewed up" their planes, choosing navigators, air gunners and others they thought would make a good team. Then they went on operations – "Ops."

An RCAF pilot asked Jim Lovelace if he would like to join his crew soon after the WOP/AG arrived at No 11 OTU in Bassingbourne in England. Lovelace readily agreed, but the pilot died that night while doing "circuits and bumps" – a take-off and landing exercise. On his third day at OTU Lovelace went on a training flight in a Wellington bomber and then learned he would be going on his first mission on the same evening. He replaced an "over wrought front gunner", wondering "what if it be my first and last flight?" Lovelace later flew with the nervous gunner who managed to conquer his fears. If an airman suddenly refused to fly on Ops, and became a waverer, he might be stood down and given time to regain his nerve. Or he might have LMF ("Lack of Moral Fibre") stamped on his papers, be stripped of his rank and assigned to menial duties.

At home, Eastern Air Command (EAC) covered the Maritimes and stretched from Eastern Québec to Newfoundland, scouting for U-boats in the North Atlantic. The official history of the RCAF noted that its senior officers "were overly parochial in outlook and too often failed to get their priorities right" refusing to co-operate with the Royal Canadian Navy (RCN). Arguments developed over the role of aircraft in the sea war off Canada's coasts. Were they simply to fly cover for convoys – or hunt and kill enemy submarines?

S/L "Molly" Small of 113 Squadron believed in aggressive action. In July 1942, while piloting a Hudson, he spotted a U-boat on the surface south-east of Sable Island and dived to attack it. Four depth charges landed around U-754 and it went to the bottom. Small received the Distinguished Flying Cross (DFC), but died in a flying accident a few months later. The planes of EAC sank six U-boats and damaged three others.

Western Air Command (WAC) protected the Pacific coast but its members saw little action. When the Japanese occupied the Aleutian islands of Attu and Kiska in June 1942, RCAF fighters and bombers of WAC joined American planes in attacks on their bases. On September 23, S/L K.A. Boomer shot down a Zero, the only RCAF pilot with both Japanese and German kills to his credit.

In all commands, team work and leadership lengthened the odds of survival for those who flew. Canadians in RAF Coastal

The Westland Lysander performed numerous tasks, including taking agents into occupied Europe. SAM

Command endured hours of monotony, flying from bases such as Castle Archdale and Limavady, in Northern Ireland, Sullum Voe, in the Shetlands, and Reykjavik, in Iceland, in search of enemy submarines. Sometimes the U-boats dived, at other times they put up a spirited defence with their cannon and machine-guns. On their first op, the crew of a Sunderland of Canadian 422 Squadron fought a brisk battle with U-625 off Northern Ireland. The boat's guns peppered the seaplane and its crew plugged the holes with chewing gum.

On June 24, 1944, F/L David Hornell, piloting a Catalina amphibian, attacked a submarine near the Faroes. Pressing on through flak, Hornell sank the U-boat. The starboard engine fell off as Hornell and his co-pilot, Bernard Denomy, brought the Catalina down on the water where it began to sink. The eight crew members scrambled into the only undamaged dinghy as the seas began to rise. Two died before a rescue launch reached them 21 hours later. Hornell died on board it. He had completed 60 missions and received a posthumous VC for "valour and devotion to duty of the highest order."

J.K. Chapman also served in Coastal Command and described himself as a "survivor." Enlisting in the RCAF in November 1940, Chapman trained as a navigator and served in torpedo and bomb-carrying Hampdens of 415 Squadron. In June and July 1942, it lost six aircaft. Only one crew member survived after spending 14 days in a dinghy in the North Sea. This man had both legs amputated after rescue. Chapman married before leaving Canada and returned there after a year on Ops. He left home a boy and returned a man – grey-haired, 15 kg underweight, fingers stained with nicotine, unable to sleep at nights.

Most Canadians served in Fighter and Bomber Commands, sometimes with RAF squadrons, but increasingly, as the war continued, with their fellow-countrymen in the RCAF. When the war began, about a thousand Canadians were either in the RAF or training as aircrew. Some of these "CAN/RAF" men joined the first all-Canadian fighter squadron, No 242. It came into being at Church Fenton, Yorkshire, on October 30, 1939. Most of the pilots had paid to acquire their licences, and included a bank clerk, a bandleader, a gold miner, a medical student and civil engineer. The Hurricanes of 242 Squadron flew to a field near Nantes as the Canadian 1st Brigade advanced into France in the spring of 1940. From here, the pilots tried to protect the troops on the beaches of Dunkirk. By May 10, it had 22 flyers on strength and had shot down 30 enemy planes for a loss of seven men killed, three captured and three wounded. As the brigade withdrew, so did 242 Squadron.

A naval officer briefs airmen at Eastern Air Command. Brigadier-General P.D. Lloyd

As the war progressed, senior Canadian officers and politicians battled with commanders in the RAF who wanted to control Canadian fighter and bomber squadrons. On June 24, 1940, S/L Douglas Bader took command of 242 Squadron and began to rebuild its morale. Bader lost both legs in an accident in 1931, but persuaded the RAF to take him back into the service. An aggressive, innovative leader and a completely fearless man, he provided an excellent example for the pilots of 242. Eventually, it had very few Canadian members and went to Sumatra in March 1942 where the Japanese wiped it out.

In June 1940, Canada's No. 1 Squadron arrived at Middle Wallop. On August 15, S/L E.A. McNab shot down a German Dornier to claim the RCAF's first victory. Eleven days later, NcNab and two companions fell to the guns of enemy planes. McNab and one pilot survived, but F/O R.L. Edwards became the first RCAF member to die in aerial combat.

A plane from Eastern Air Command attacks a submarine off the coast of Canada. SAM

The poet W.H. Auden called pilots "the closest modern equivalent to the Homeric hero." British propaganda played up the "devil-may-care" image of fighter pilots who went around with the top button of their tunics undone to show defiance of authority and became known as "Brylcreem Boys" from the hair cream they were all alleged to use.

No. 1 Squadron fought in the Battle of Britain, which lasted from July 10 to October 31, 1940. The Germans tried to knock out fighter bases and radar warning systems in preparation for an invasion of England. The life expectancy of a fighter pilot during this battle was 87 flying hours, or about two weeks. Its numbers reduced by flu, No. 1 Squadron sought to beat off enemy air attacks on Britain in two months of constant action. In late September, the squadron medical officer reported: "There is a definite air of constant tension and they are unable to relax as they are on constant call. The pilots go to work with forced enthusiasm and appear to be suffering from strain and general tiredness..."

In the fall, as the weather deteriorated, No. 1 Squadron went to Scotland, ending up, in December, in miserable quarters in Thurso.

As new Canadian squadrons formed in Britain, their pilots confronted experienced German veterans of the Luftwaffe flying faster and more manoeuverable machines. By the end of 1941, the five Canadian squadrons in Britain claimed only 22 victories between them. Some of the pilots converted to Spitfires. On October 27, the Luftwaffe shot down five of them and damaged two others, with little loss to themselves. On a sweep over France on June 21, 1942, 403 Squadron lost eight of its planes in a sudden, swift attack by enemy fighters.

RCAF senior NCOs of No. 10 (Bomber Reconnaissance) with Liberator. SAM

A rocket-firing Beaufighter of 404 Squadron in Banff, Scotland, in 1944. SAM

Early in 1943, W/C Johnnie Johnson, who became the Commonwealth's highest scoring ace, took over 402 Squadron. He had learned much from Douglas Bader and passed on his knowledge about team flying to his pilots. Johnson wrote: "I found the Canadians first-class chaps, a well-disciplined outfit. Canadians are hunters…Even the city men were hunters, outdoor men. They were always clamouring to go."

The squadron acquired Mark IX Spitfires and Johnson's reaction to these powerful machines echoed what Canadian pilots must have thought: "I'm going to live…We've got the machine that will see them off."

Johnson decided that it would be wrong for an Englishman to discipline Canadians and left that duty to his squadron commanders. He also recognized a problem that marked Canadian leadership: "When I arrived the Canadians hadn't been terribly well led; they'd had a Wing Commander who wasn't a very aggressive sort of chap." This officer had run a training wing, and Johnson commented: "That was one of the faults of the Canadians – they brought these middle-ranking chaps…straight from Canada into operational jobs, and they usually fell down."

Johnson got on so well with Canadians that his pilots invited him to wear the "Canada" flash on the shoulder of his uniform. As he put it: "The Canadians thought I was OK."

But one man presented the Englishman – and other officers – with continual problems because of his individualistic behaviour.

George "Buzz" Beurling, also known as "Screwball", flew at the age of nine and soloed at 16. Rejected by the RCAF in Canada because he did not graduate from high school, Beurling hopped on a ship to Britain and joined the RAF in 1940. On May 3, 1942, while over Calais, the Canadian peeled off from his formation to attack and destroy the leader of a squadron of German planes. Landing later at the base, he received a frosty reception from the other pilots for failing to cover his companion's tail. "That's not done, old man", his commander told Beurling.

Posted to 249 Squadron in Malta, the Canadian downed 27 German and Italian aircraft, damaged eight others and scored three probables in the summer of 1942. Speaking to RCAF intakes, Beurling told of blowing the head off an Italian pilot. A natural and reckless flyer and skilled shot, he had that sixth sense that marks great fighter pilots. "You have to be hard hearted", Beurling said. But he admitted to his sister that he saw the faces of the men he killed. On October 14, 1942, Beurling's luck ran out when he failed to look behind him as he went into an attack. Wounded and shot down, Beurling was rescued and returned to Canada a hero, with a commission, the DSO, DFM and Bar. Billy Bishop described him as "Canada's young falcon of Malta." Back in action in Britain, Beurling added three more enemy planes to his score for a total of 31 1/3, making him the highest scoring Canadian ace. Johnnie Johnson described him as "a difficult man", but felt, "we had to give him a chance—after all, he had lots of medals…[but] we couldn't make a team player out of him." After take off, the

A Canadian pilot and his Typhoon of a front line RCAF squadron in Normandy. NAC

Canadian would do a half-roll and disappear. Johnson wrote: "I could do nothing with him. We should have given him a long-range Mustang and said, 'OK, go off and fight your own private war.'" Transferring to 403 Squadron in September 1943, Beurling helped young pilots to improve their marksmanship. Resenting any form of discipline, he left the RCAF in October 1944, dying in a mysterious plane crash in Rome while on his way to fight for Israel, on May 20, 1948.

One source described Canadians as, "bush pilots in uniform", who worked easily with people on the ground. They came into their own in the Tactical Air Force formed to prepare the way for the Normandy invasion and to attack enemy targets after it. This meant co-operating with advancing army units.

Canadian pilots flew numerous sorties, shooting at anything that moved in France, attacking enemy troops, vehicles, positions, trains and other targets.

Before D-Day, RCAF Spitfires escorted American and RAF medium bombers that blasted German airfields, transportation systems, coastal defences and "Noball" sites being prepared for launching V-1 rocket bombs on England. After the Allies landed, RCAF units with No. 83 Group supported the troops of the British Second Army in its thrust through France. Small formations of fighters and fighter bombers hovered above the soldiers in "cab ranks." They could be called down for immediate tactical support to obliterate obstacles holding up the advance of troops. RCAF pilots swooped down on German troops and transport heading for the Falaise Gap, giving the retreating enemy no quarter.

By now, Canadian pilots had become highly skilled in combat and attack. The nine Canadian squadrons claimed 262 victories with very few losses in the three months after June 6. Seven days after the landings, however, W/C Chadburn and another pilot died in a collision. On October

The P-51 Mustang flown by five RCAF squadrons during the war and 12 auxiliary squadrons postwar, including 402 (City of Winnipeg) Squadron. SAM

5, five pilots of 401 Squadron, led by S/L R.I.A. Smith shot down an ME 262 jet bomber – the first kill of a new and much faster plane. Flying a Spitfire, F/L Dick Audet of 411 Squadron brought down five German planes on a single sortie on December 29, 1944. He died two months later, hit by flak while attacking a train.

On January 1, 1945, the Luftwaffe made one last, desperate effort to cripple Allied air power by launching an attack on their airfields. At Eindhoven in Holland, the RCAF lost 31 planes, 13 pilots killed and many more wounded. The strike at Heesch, however, failed to catch any Canadian planes on the ground, and the groundcrew fought back. Sgt. W.L. Lang of 438 Squadron and F/Sgt. McGee decided to "take a whack at anything flying over dispersal" with Bren guns and shot down an enemy fighter.

As a 20-year old pilot, Richard Rohmer flew a Mustang on reconnaissance before D-Day. Although he claimed to have a "gung ho" attitude and believed himself invincible, the Canadian admitted to having "a bit of a twitch" as he flew towards Dieppe on April 24, 1944. The Spitfires ahead of him attacked shipping in the harbour, then Rohmer came in to photograph the results, suddenly aware that all the flak guns were shooting at him. He took the photographs, but only one of them came out – and it showed nothing of importance. Unaware of their significance, Rohmer took pictures of "Noball" sites near St. Omer for bombers. Then he spotted targets for Canadian and British troops, calling down rocket-firing Typhoons and bomb-carrying Spitfires on the retreating enemy as the Allies swept through France.

Rohmer survived the war.

Norman Fowlow, a Newfoundlander, did not. After serving in Malta, where he was shot down on his second sortie, the pilot flew sweeps in a Spitfire fighter-bomber over France. On May 19, 1944, Fowlow attacked a railway crossing at Hazebruck. Flak hit his plane, exploding the 200 kg bomb below it and the Spitfire blew up.

F/O Adam, a RAF pilot, recalled what happened on "normal operations" over France. He saw a Typhoon, flown by Canadian Piwi Williams, begin to lose height and radioed him: "What are you doing?" The Canadian replied that he was hit and paralyzed. His last words before his plane crashed were: "Order me a late tea." Adam continually wondered at "how some people died, being fully aware that they were going to die."

From a slow and confused start, Canadian fighter pilots, with superior planes and skilled team work, began to survive and to best their tough and determined enemies. Some, like W/C Hugh Godefroy, S/L Wally McLeod, S/L E.A. McNab, W/C "Buck" McNair, W/C "Les" Ford and W/C "Moose" Fumerton scored more than five victories and became aces. Ford died while attacking a German ship on June 4, 1943. While patrolling beyond the Rhine on September 27, 1944, McLeod failed to turn in time and a Bf 109 shot him down. The pilot's remains, still in his Spitfire, were recovered by advancing Canadian troops.

Life in Bomber Command was very different from the split-second existence of

A fighter takes off from a temporary landing strip after the invasion of Europe. NAC

fighter pilots. Team work in a crew was vital. As a saying put it: "The crew that flies together, fights together and drinks together, survives together." And it was in the skies above Europe that most Canadian airmen died. On some missions the casualties exceeded those of Canadian pilots in the Battle of Britain. In early January 1992, CBC broadcast three revisionist programmes on the Second World War. Two dealt with Canadian disasters at Hong Kong and Verrières Ridge, and the third with Bomber Command. This segment of *The Valour and the Horror* created a storm of controversy. The armchair experts who made it implied that the sole aim of Canadians in Bomber Command was to murder innocent German women and children. This claim was rebutted vigorously by those who had served in Bomber Command. The programme failed to point out that the Germans initiated the bombing of civilians. On May 14, 1940, German bombers destroyed 2.8 sq. km of the centre of Rotterdam, killing between 800 and 980 civilians, to force the Dutch to capitulate. The Allies threatened to retaliated against their cities if the Germans bombed civilian targets. The strategic air offensive against Germany began with a raid on the Ruhr, on May 15, 1940. As one veteran of Bomber Command put it they "dished out the dirt when no one else on our side could." When the Germans occupied Europe in 1940, Britain stood alone, and its air force offered the only way to strike at the enemy.

The head of Bomber Commander, Air Chief Marshal Harris, believed that Germany could be brought to its knees by attacks on strategic targets from the air that would cripple its industrial capacity. Initially, the missions often proved fruitless as bombs landed outside the designated targets. With improvements in aircraft, tactics and technology, the planes of Bomber Command increasingly hit their targets with precision. And still the casualties mounted.

On December 18, 1939, Bomber Command sent 22 planes against Wangerooge in the Frisian Islands. Only ten returned. Even as the war in Europe ended, airmen still died in large numbers. On April 25, 1945, a bomber force again attacked Wangerooge. It lost seven planes, six because of collisions, and 28 Canadian and 13 British airmen died.

The controversy over the Bomber Command segment in the CBC programme diverted attention from the bravery of the Canadians who took to the air, night after night, to fly for hours over a hostile land in search of their targets. They dropped "Window", strips of aluminum foil, to neutralize radar-directed interceptors and fired false signal flares to convince Germans on the ground that they were on their side. New radar systems like IFF, GEE and H2S enabled them to see their targets in the dark and return home safely. The Germans also improved their radar and interception tactics. The B17 Flying Fortresses of the United States Air Force, which carried out daylight missions, had belly turrets. Bomber Command's planes lacked them, and German fighters would move under them and play *Schräge Musik* ("oblique" or jazz music) pouring fire from their upward pointing guns into the lumbering plane above them. First hand accounts from Bomber Command tell of planes simply exploding in mid-air. Some were "coned" by enemy searchlights and then shot down by radar-controlled guns.

The first Canadian bomber squadron came into existence in June 1941. RCAF bombers took part in Operation Millennium on May 30, 1942. More than a thousand bombers set off for Cologne, including 71 from the RCAF. Three fifths of the bombs fell within 6 km of the aiming point: The raid cost Bomber Command 41 aircraft. Many Canadians had been in British cities when the Germans bombed them, and as one participant in the raid put it: "We really made up for the blitzing of London and added some."

In addition to attacking enemy targets, the Canadians had to fight the British to establish their own bomber group. "Chubby" Power, the Minister of National Defence (Air), insisted that Canadians run their own show. On January 1, 1943, No. 6 (RCAF) Group Bomber Command came into being with eight squadrons scattered throughout Yorkshire: this number would eventually rise to 14. Night after night, bombers rose into the skies and set off for enemy targets. Power implemented a policy in early 1944 whereby all air crew held commissioned rank, a move that a British historian claimed had "both logic and humanity" on its side.

Canada had few officers skilled in commanding bomber squadrons and No. 6 Group did not fare well in its first year. Its planes had a greater distance to fly to targets than those based further south in Britain. And while No. 6 Group did receive new aircraft, many of the crews served their time in Wellingtons, a sturdy, twin-engined plane with a geodetic frame that could take much punishment. In typical service fashion, those who flew "Wimpys" – named for a character in Popeye cartoons – made up a rude song to the tune of "Bless 'Em All." It began "Worry me, worry me, /Wellingtons don't worry me" and continued with unprintable details of the planes' shortcomings. No 6 Group had a loss rate of 7 per cent (100 bombers) between March 5 and June 24. Canadians distinguished themselves in the RAF. On the first mission in the Battle of Berlin on August 23, 1943, a Ju88 fired on a Stirling, wounding the pilot. The bomb aimer, John Bailey, a Canadian who almost completed his pilot training before being "washed out", took over the controls and brought the bomber back to base. He received an immediate commission and the award of the Conspicuous Gallantry Medal.

Early in 1944, Air Vice Marshal C.M. "Black Mike" McEwen, MC, DFC, "a demon for training and standards", took command of No.6 Group. He had been a fighter pilot

A Lancaster Bomber: 7000 of these were made during the war. SAM

in the First World War, serving on the Italian Front, downing 27 enemy planes. A forceful personality and strict disciplinarian, McEwen flew on missions with his men and the morale in the Group began to rise as the casualties dropped.

Heroism became commonplace as bombers soared across the flak-strewn, fighter-infested skies. Two Canadians in Bomber Command won the Victoria Cross. Just before setting out to bomb railyards at Cambrai in France on June 12, 1944, Warrant Officer Second Class (later Pilot Officer) Andrew Mynarski found a four-leaf clover. Mynarski, the mid-upper gunner on a Lancaster, gave it to his friend Pat Brophy, the rear-gunner. Fighters attacked the bomber, knocking out two engines and setting it on fire. The pilot ordered the crew to bail out and Mynarski headed for the escape hatch. Then he saw Brophy trapped in his turret. With his clothes and parachute alight, his friend tried to free him, without success. Brophy gestured for Mynarski to save himself. At the escape hatch, he turned, stood to attention, saluted his friend, then bailed out, so badly burned that he died soon after. Brophy miraculously survived the crash of the Lancaster and told of his friends' heroic attempt to save him. Mynarski received the VC.

Pathfinder squadrons led the way to targets and marked them for the main bomber force. On August 4, 1944, S/L Ian Bazalgette piloted the master bomber on an attack on Trossy St. Maximin. Flak hit the Lancaster as it approached the target, knocking out the starboard engines and setting it on fire. Bazalgette pressed on, marked the target and bombed it accurately.

As he turned for home, the bomber headed towards the ground. Bazalgette brought the plane under control and ordered his crew to bail out. All did so, except the wounded bomb aimer and the mid-upper gunner who had been overcome by smoke. Bazalgette landed the bomber safely, but it blew up, killing all three airmen: he received a posthumous VC.

Numerous accounts tell of pilots holding their planes steady so that their crews could bail out, well aware that they would not survive. F/L Gordon Thring of 620 Squadron, piloted a Stirling towing gliders of the 6th Airborne Division to land troops near Caen on D-Day. After releasing the glider, the plane, hit by flak, flipped over on its back. As one crew member put it: "Because of the 'G' pressure, we were in a position to do absolutely nothing." Thring pulled back on the stick, and the plane suddenly "came over off its back and we made a beautiful belly-landing in a ploughed field that would have done justice to any pilot under normal circumstances." The crew walked away uninjured before the aircraft exploded and Thring won a DFC.

Awards of medals marked singular acts of courage in the air by Canadians. Jim Lovelace recalled disciplining a young WOP/AG at a Reception Wing who claimed to be 17. He had feigned drunkenness and waded into the CO's fish pond as a ploy to be posted to an OTU. Lovelace obliged and the man left on the next draft. On the following day, Lovelace received a priority letter from a mother seeking to have her son, aged 14, released from the RCAF. This was the air gunner who had just left the station. He returned a week later and Lovelace confronted him. The 14-year-old had arrived on an RCAF station and gone on a "Channel nursery trip" on the following day. Then he flew to the Ruhr, shot down two German fighters and proudly showed Lovelace the ribbon of the DFM he had won. After receiving the medal at Buckingham Palace, the boy was back in Canada a few days later.

Lovelace won his DFC for bravery after his Wellington crashed on the night of September 9-10, 1942. After bombing Russelheim, the plane caught flak which smashed the radio equipment. Lovelace jury-rigged a transmitter, enabling the pilot to receive directions from his base. As he tried to land, "a ground object suddenly appeared…Both engines cut and the aircraft crashed into a large tree at 04:00…" in the words of the Air Ministry report. The plane burst into flames and the second pilot and front gunner died. Lovelace ended up in hospital with amnesia, learning later that he had been commissioned and awarded the DFC for "Courage, Skill and Devotion to Duty." The crash ended his flying career.

Doug Harvey, a sergeant pilot, went on his first mission as an observer. His plane crossed the belt of searchlights and anti aircraft guns on the French coast, lost one engine and bombed Gelsenkirchen. On the return from the target, a night fighter knocked out another engine. Harvey suggested restarting the engine that had been shut down and it burst into life. The Canadian took off on his last mission on March 30, 1944, in an 800 bomber force headed for Nuremberg. Bomber Command lost 97 aircraft on that raid. When Harvey returned he heard the magic words: "You're screened." He had finished his tour.

Dave McIntosh aptly summarized his war experiences in the title of his book, *Terror in the Starboard Seat*. He flew 41 missions in a Mosquito, a very fast, twin-engined fighter bomber. Canadian factories turned out large numbers of these planes. Made of plywood, they became known as the "Termite's Delight" and the "Wooden Wonder." McIntosh and his pilot Sid Seid chased and shot down V-1 rockets, and patrolled German airfields at night attacking planes as they took off and landed. He compared flak to orange, yellow and red tennis balls that seemed to come through the nose of his plane. By the end of the war, No. 6 Group had become one of the most effective in Bomber Command, with the lowest casualties. Its planes had flown 41,000 sorties, dropping 126,000 tons of bombs at a cost of 814 aircraft and 3,500 air crew killed in action. Canadian casualties in Bomber Command totalled 9,980 of whom 8,290 died on operations.

After the end of the war, W/C Angus MacLean, who later became premier of Prince Edward Island, had the melancholy task of searching for missing airmen. After two years of research he wrote: "Of the 3,500 cases our unit solved while I was in Europe, none had a happy ending. We found not a single instance in which a missing airman was still alive."

The pattern that emerges from the history of Canadians in the air war shows a number of characteristics: initial enthusiasm followed by the grim realization of what flying in combat involved; declines in morale, then the emergence of strong, skilled leadership and the slow realization that their side would win.

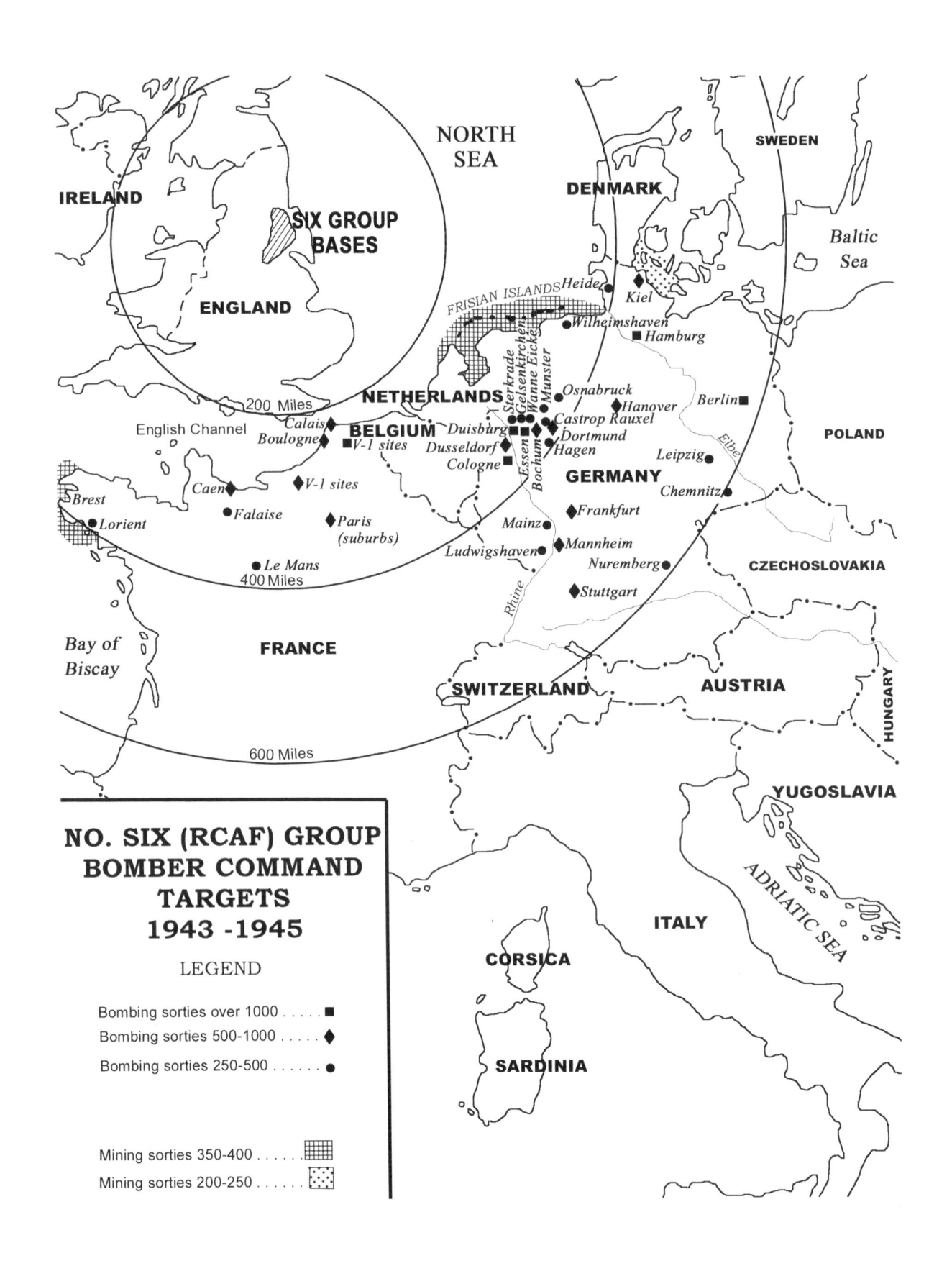

NO. SIX (RCAF) GROUP BOMBER COMMAND TARGETS 1943-1945

LEGEND

Bombing sorties over 1000 .... ■
Bombing sorties 500-1000 .... ♦
Bombing sorties 250-500 .... ●

Mining sorties 350-400 .... ▦
Mining sorties 200-250 .... ▨

The air war created its own language, symbols, and rituals. Planes did not crash – they "pranged." Pilots did not die – they "bought it." Wild parties and strange games in the messes served as wakes for lost comrades. Airmen became superstitious and developed routines to ward off danger and death. Some peed on the rear wheel of their aircraft before take-off. Others carried soft toys or lucky articles of clothing on operations. F/O Gus Utas of 427 Squadron took Ruthless Robert, a small stuffed lion, the animal after whom the squadron was named, when he flew. Another airman always wore an old hockey sweater.

Fear rode with them all the time.

As one bomber pilot put it: "Although death always lurked on our doorstep, we tried not to dwell too much on our personal danger." Like many others, he clung to the notion that "we were not going to die. Death would always come to the other guy." Nevertheless, he admitted that "most of us did a lot of praying."

A warning posted in many messes and ready rooms stated: "There are old pilots, and bold pilots; there are no old, bold pilots."

Canadian flyers soon discovered that surviving in the sky depended on team work, leadership and continuous learning. Fighter pilots had a greater degree of freedom in the air, scrambling to attack enemy planes or waiting for their approach, and going on "rhubarbs", freelance sorties, shooting up selective targets. Their lives consisted of short, sharp encounters with the enemy on the ground and in the air. Bomber crews formed cohesive teams, with each member looking out for the other and conquering their fears while doing so. Walter Thompson saw pilots arrive at his squadron, looking like scared rabbits. They disappeared quickly. He recorded how stimulated he felt on missions, more afraid of showing cowardice than of suffering death. Some targets such as Berlin inspired fear at briefings. Units with poor morale suffered higher casualties than those that developed skills in working together. Molly Small, one of the most successful pilots in Eastern Air Command, studied the reports from other units engaged in anti-submarine warfare. Many other air crew relaxed after missions and failed to keep on learning all they could about their tasks. Bomber crews had to understand their planes and their equipment

A Lancaster takes off somewhere in England. SAM

– and their companions – to be effective in the air.

Many Canadians flew in mixed crews drawn from all over the Commonwealth and Britain. Walter Thompson flew as "second dickie" (pilot) in a RAF bomber on his first Op on March 11, 1943, at the age of 22. The bomb aimer was a naval officer, and the captain made Thompson responsible for monitoring the fuel consumption. In the air, Thompson, feeling secure in the company of experts, "witnessed a phenomenon that was new to me. Twinkling little lights." The captain identified them as "Enemy coast. Flak – probably Cherbourg." The Lancaster lost two engines to flak, dropped its bombs on Stuttgart and returned to base: "…our landing was more in the nature of a controlled crash." Thompson became a Pathfinder, and survived his tour, writing of his experiences in *Lancaster to Berlin*. He noted that "throughout my operations I never hated a single German, and had no hatred for them as a people." Like Murray Peden's *A Thousand Shall Fall*, Thompsons' book catches the feel of the naked fear of those who served in bombers. Peden looked back at his service with 214 Squadron as "a time both wonderful and terrible", recalling, "the repressed fear of having to fly yet again through bursting flak, prowling night fighters, and the blinding glare of searchlights."

A Canadian bomber pinpoints a bridge in enemy territory.

W/C "Buck" McNair won the DSO, and the DFC and two bars for shooting down 16 enemy planes. DND

Some Canadian air crew survived against the odds and returned to Canada. Others went missing on their first op. Paul Métivier, a First World War veteran recalled his son Roland, an RCAF air gunner, lost off the coast of France: "He was just gone. They never found the airplane. None of the crew. There were no bodies. They never came back." F/O Doug Smith, known as "Daddy" to his crew, served with a Beaufort Torpedo squadron. His plane went down, but he survived the crash only to die of wounds in a POW camp. A street in Halifax is named after him. The monument to Commonwealth aircrew at Runnymede in England carries the names of 20,000 lost airmen, including 3,050 from Canada and 25 from Newfoundland.

Some crews bailed out of flaming aircraft, landed safely and spent the rest of the war in a *Stalag Luft*, a prisoner of war camp for airmen. On March 24-25, 1944, 76 Allied airmen took part in "The Great Escape," an event mythologized by Hollywood. Wally Floody had been a miner in Kirkland Lake, Ontario, before the war, and supervised the digging of escape tunnels that led out of *Stalag Luft* III, which lay 100 kms northeast of Berlin. Only three prisoners escaped. Hitler ordered 50 others, including six Canadian officers, shot.

Angus MacLean "made it home," although the six other members of his Halifax, H for Harry, ended up in prison camps. On June 8, 1942, on a trip to the Krupps works in Essen, the plane was coned by searchlights and flak exploded all around it, throwing the Halifax into a spin. MacLean regained control and flew on to bomb the target. Then a stream of cannon shells shattered the plane, crippling it. Over Holland, MacLean weighed the chances of

A Halifax Bomber displays its total of raids on its nose. SAM.

reaching his base, facing a "horribly, difficult decision" as the plane lost power and headed for the ground: "I was responsible not only for my own life, but for the lives of the other six crew members, all of them fine young men." Holding the plane steady, he ordered his crew to bail out, then dived out of the escape hatch a few hundred feet above the ground and landed in the middle of a herd of Holstein cows. MacLean evaded capture for 72 days. The Comet Line took him and other downed Allied airmen through Holland, Belgium, France and over the Pyrenees into Spain. Many people in occupied Europe helped the evaders, and many paid with their lives for doing so.

All who flew knew that the performance of their planes and their chances of survival depended on the skills and dedication of ground crews. Robert Collins, who grew up on a farm near Shamrock, Saskatchewan, recorded his life as a fitter in *The Long and the Short and the Tall*. He spent several months at a small station in Mont Joli, Québec, before being posted to No. 6 Bomber Group at Wombleton in James Herriot country just as the war ended. Here he discovered "the magic of British pubs" and the sheer inedibility of English food, revelling in the friendship he experienced with men and women from all over Canada. On June 16, 1945, Collins wrote home, noting that : "We have a few kites to look after but as they don't fly there isn't any work." Carrying rifles and Sten guns and ammunition, Collins and his comrades moved in September to Hamburg to service the Spitfires of RCAF 126 Wing on a former Luftwaffe base. He saw a pilot crash when his engine cut out after take off, and thought: "What a stupid waste, that he should die in this nonwar."

The Second World War changed the face of Canada, as training centres sprang up and men came from all over the world to learn the trades of aerial warfare. Airfields built in the Eastern Arctic and along the Alaska Highway opened up the North.

And those who served in the air war returned to Canada, changed in ways they could never have imagined. Collins described himself as a "winner" because he had "that rare opportunity to glimpse the world, and grow…I had learned to live and cope. The war had helped me and thousands of others break out of the trap of the Depression." He did not count himself among the "glittering minority" who flew. Murray Peden, one of them, looked back on his time in combat and reflected: "It was wonderful in the sense that never is fragile life so precious and rewarding as when we cannot count on savouring it for more than another day, one more Battle Order."

While lamenting the loss of friends, Peden recognized that he had gained an entirely new perspective on life, and a

---

Airmen of Eastern Air Command relax after an "op". JBB

"marvellous measuring rod that shrinks subsequent trials."

In typical, modest, Canadian fashion, he adds:

"And sometimes, secretly, a man cannot help feeling a little proud that he had paid the the high price of admission, and can walk unchallenged in the company of a small group of similarly-tested brothers.

In His own way, God favoured us richly."

Pvt Elbert Pieper on sentry duty near a trapper's cabin used as a store holding material for the Alaska Highway. NAC

AT SEA

"Under the terrible testing of the elements and an unseen enemy, a whole new set of standards emerged, far different from those we had accepted in the comfortable world of peace."

James B. Lamb, *On The Triangle Run.*

Canada entered the Second World War with six destroyers, a handful of smaller ships and 3,800 sailors in the Royal Canadian Navy (RCN), the Royal Canadian Naval Reserve (RCNR) and the Royal Canadian Naval Volunteer Reserve. The RCNR, established in 1923, had a few hundred members drawn from maritime occupations. The "Wavy Navy," the RCNVR, consisted of part-time sailors. Set up in the same year as the RCNR, it derived its name from the wavy stripes on the cuffs of the uniforms of its officers.

By the end of hostilities, Canada's navy had become the third largest among the Allies, with 900 vessels, including 375 combat ships. In all, 106,522 sailors, including 6,781 members of the Women's Royal Canadian Naval Service, wore navy blue. The RCN lost 24 ships and some 2,200 sailors during the war, and sank 27 U-boats on its own or in co-operation with other ships and planes. The RCN also destroyed or captured 42 enemy surface ships.

Canadian sailors fought in the broad Atlantic and in the narrow seas of Europe in small vessels - destroyers, frigates, corvettes, minesweepers, motor torpedo boats, and landing craft. They served on the Murmansk Run to Russia and in the Caribbean and the Mediterranean. RCN corvettes and landing craft took part in Operation Torch, the invasion of North Africa in 1942. Desperately short of ships and sailors, the RCN accepted seamen with experience anywhere it could. Jack Gillingham, a Newfoundlander, spent 17 years in the Merchant Navy and hastened to enlist when war broke out. A naval officer looked at his discharge book and said: "You're in. You're the kind we need." A medical examination found a large pleurisy scar on Gillingham's lungs. Three days after volunteering, the Newfoundlander was on a ship, without any training, patrolling Canada's east coast.

HMCS *Esquimault*. MCM

A depth charge thrower – and the results. MCM.

On shore, Canada's volunteer sailors had to understand and conform to the ways of the "pusser" (proper) navy. Afloat they entered an egalitarian world where everyone had to look out for his fellows in crowded ships in perilous seas. As one captain put it: "We had two enemies: the U-boats and the weather. I often wondered which was worse."

Corvettes formed the backbone of the RCN. In February, 1940, the Canadian government ordered 64 of these small ships, known officially as "Patrol Vessels, Whaler Type." They presented challenges to Canadian shipyards. The first vessels of the Flower Class, 63 metres long, had a range of 6,436 km, at 12 knots and were very manoeuvrable. After the Flower Class came ships named for Canadian cities, and by the end of the war 122 corvettes had been built in Canada. The crews, comprising 47 officers and men, lived in cramped quarters that became even more crowded when new technologies for anti-submarine warfare were installed and new specialists came aboard.

Corvettes proved to be wet ships, never dry, forever shipping water that rolled around the decks and flooded the messes. They iced up quickly in winter and crews had to hack away the accretions to keep the corvettes stable. These little ships rocked and rolled, and the prairie boys and city clerks who manned them became seasick. But they did their duty, never letting their shipmates down. The armaments of the corvettes consisted of a 4-inch gun, a 2-pounder pom-pom, and a few machine-guns. But they had teeth in the form of depth charges that could be dropped off the stern or fired from throwers on each side of the ship. The main role of corvettes involved protecting convoys struggling across the Atlantic. Serving on one of these small ships in 1941, Frank Curry wrote: "What a miserable, rotten, hopeless life…an Atlantic so rough it seems impossible that we can continue to take this unending pounding and still remain in one piece…hanging on to a convoy is a full-time job…the crew in almost a stupor from the nightmarishness of it all…and still we go on hour after hour."

Death came suddenly to the ships and men of the RCN.

L.B. "Yogi" Jenson served on HMCS *Ottawa*, a River Class destroyer protecting convoys sailing between St. John's, Newfoundland and Londonderry in Northern Ireland. He recalled a five-day storm that drove the warship back almost 350 km as it steamed at 12 knots. With another destroyer and four corvettes, *Ottawa* sailed to join a convoy of 31 ships on September 5, 1942. A U-boat "wolf pack" of 13 submarines awaited them, torpedoing four ships on one day. *Ottawa* and the corvette HMCS *St. Croix* stopped to pick up survivors from a tanker, a nerve-wracking task: "One presented a sitting target and the Germans had no compassion."

On September 13, around 11 in the evening, U-91, on its first operation, launched a torpedo that hit *Ottawa*, blowing off its

HMCS *Ottawa*. MCM

bow. Jenson recalled "an amazing geranium-coloured flash, followed by a great pillar of water which went straight up." Her engines stopped, the destroyer lay dead in the water, gently rocking. Jenson went below to check on damage and found sailors terribly wounded - - "it was like a scene out of hell."

food. Karl Doenitz, commander of the German U-Boat fleet, had been a submariner in the First World War. Germany had only 57 U-boats when war began, 27 of them ocean-going vessels. Commanded and crewed by dedicated members of an élite force, they almost won the war for Germany. Winston

Another torpedo hit *Ottawa* amidships. Trapped sailors called out for help: "These were the sounds of war, when strong men became like little children, not like John Wayne." Jenson jumped overboard, clung to a spar and watched his ship sink. A gunner's mate kept up the spirits of the drifting survivors by leading them in songs from the First World War. Soaking wet, half-frozen, covered in oil, Jenson and others clambered aboard HMS *Celandine*. But 114 of their shipmates died in the sinking.

Convoys began sailing from Canadian east coast ports on September 16, 1939, under RCN protection. Soon two convoys a week left Halifax, carrying vital war supplies and

Churchill feared only one thing - - the submarine threat that could have strangled the Allied supply lines.

From 1939 to 1943, the Battle of the Atlantic raged with each side trying to gain the upper hand. With their low profiles, German submarines proved difficult to spot, especially at night. They would slip undetected into the lines of ships in convoy, target one, torpedo it and submerge before the escort ships sighted them. Convoy HX72 left port with 42 ships on September 9, 1940. As a saying at the time put it: "Happy is the convoy with no history." On the night of September 20-21, three U-boats attacked this unhappy convoy. U-99 torpedoed the tanker

A Fairmile launch. MCM

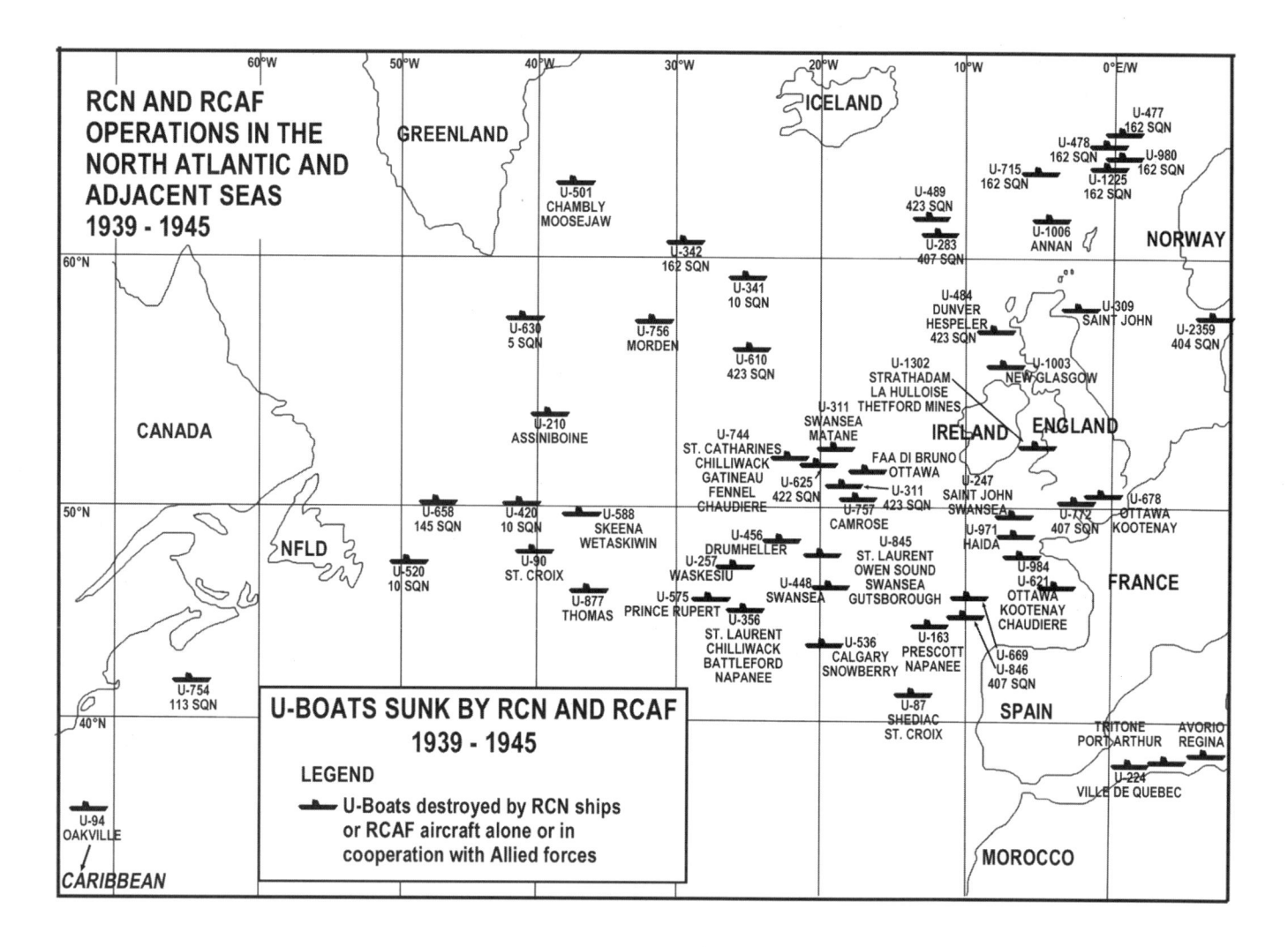

Invershannon. The crew abandoned ship, although it stayed afloat. Then the submarine sank *SS Baron Blythswood*, loaded with iron ore from Bell Island, Newfoundland. She split in two in 40 seconds, taking all but one of her crew to the ocean floor with her. U-100 and U-48 joined in the fray and the convoy lost nine more ships while its escorts dashed around frantically seeking the attackers.

After France fell in the summer of 1940, German submarines began to operate from bases like Lorient on the French Atlantic coast. German naval commanders referred to the period between January and June, 1941, as "The Happy Time." In those six months, the U-Boats sank almost three million tonnes of shipping.

When the United States entered the war in December, 1941, German submarines enjoyed another happy time. Ships sailed alone down the American coast, silhouetted against the bright lights of cities, providing easy targets for U-boats. In the first six months of 1942, they destroyed over two million tonnes of shipping for the loss of only seven boats.

By the fall of 1942, Doenitz had 300 U-boats under his command and could send

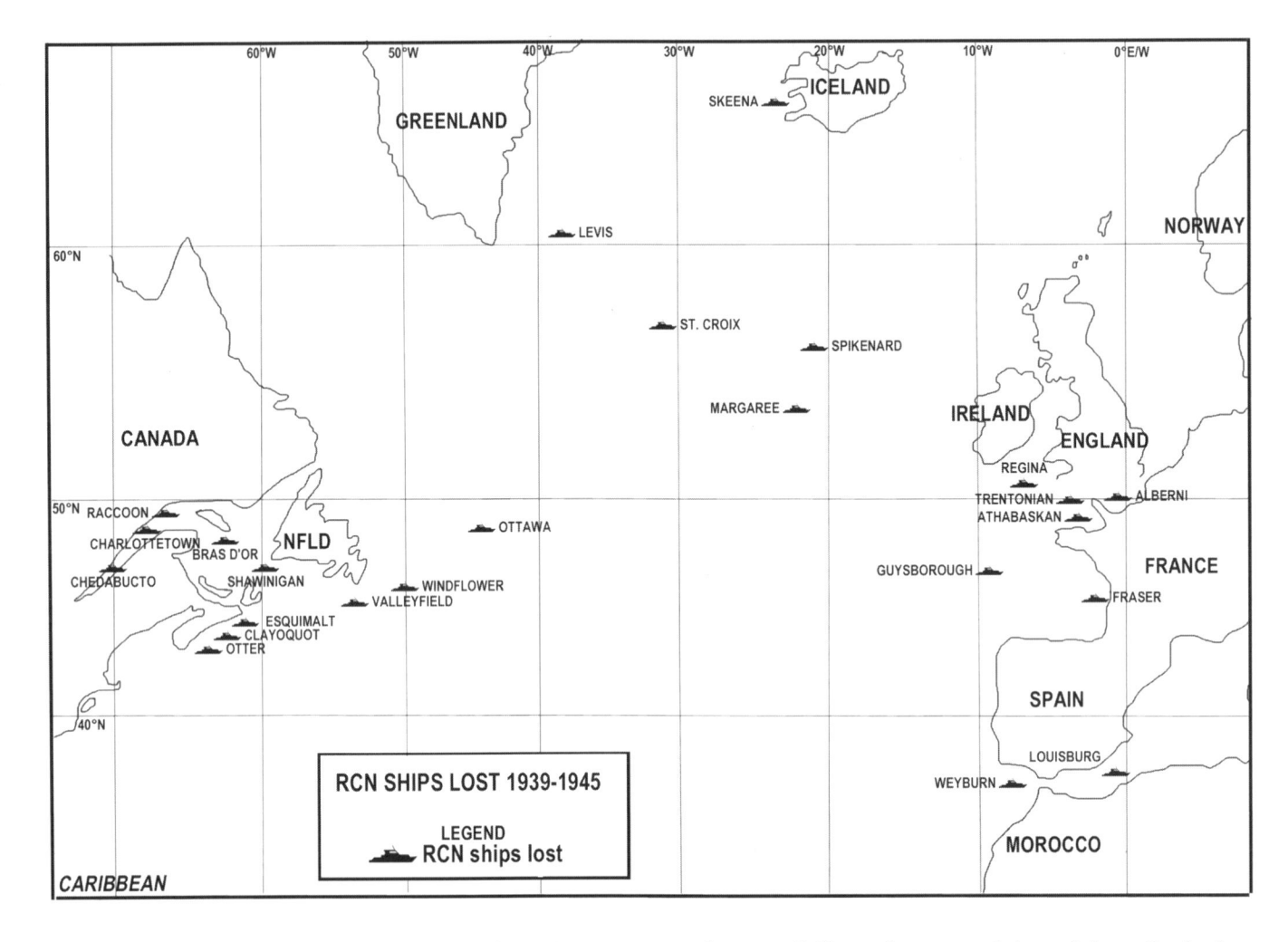

20 at a time to attack a convoy. As American ships began to sail in convoy, he sent his submarines to the Caribbean.

On August 27, 1942, the crew of HMCS *Oakville*, saw the black snout of U-94 rise out of the water south of Haiti. The corvette's captain tried to ram the submarine, but missed. The gunners hit its conning tower. Crew members sprayed the decks with Lewis guns to prevent the submariners reaching the 88 mm deck piece. As the two boats came closer, the Canadians threw Coke bottles at the enemy. Hal Lawrence, who told of this encounter in *A Bloody War*, led a boarding party. Jumping on to the deck of U-94, he advanced on the conning tower – with his shorts sliding down to his ankles. Ordering the crew on deck, Lawrence went below but discovered that the submarine was sinking. Hastily clambering out of the conning tower, Lawrence cut his elbow on a broken Coke bottle – the only Canadian to sustain an injury in the battle. Rescued by an American ship whose crew thought he was a German submariner, the Canadian officer used naval language to assert his identity. For his bravery, Lawrence won the DSO.

Early in 1942, the submarine war came to the Gulf of St. Lawrence. On the night of May 11-12, U-533 sank the British freighter *Nicoya* off the Gaspé Peninsula, and then *SS Leto*. Ottawa panicked and Naval Service

Corvette in rough seas. MCM

Headquarters announced that: "Any possible future sinkings in this area will not be made public, in order that information of value to the enemy may be withheld from him."

A Gulf Escort Force of five Bangor minesweepers, three Fairmile launches and an armed yacht, HMCS *Raccoon*, escorted convoys sailing to Sydney from Québec. Eastern Air Command stepped up its surveillance. On July 6, U-132 sank three ships in a convoy in the Gulf of St. Lawrence, then settled on the bottom while escorts sought to find her. Surfacing, the submarine torpedoed the *Frederika Lensen*.

On August 27, U-517 and U-165 waited near the entrance to the Strait of Belle Island for a suitable target. As the US troop transport *Chatham*, carrying 562 passengers, hove into view, U-517 sent her to the bottom with the loss of 13 lives. A few days later, a submarine sank HMCS *Raccoon*. The ship and her crew of 37 simply vanished, leaving no trace, save for the body of one sailor.

On September 9, 1942, the Canadian government closed the St. Lawrence to all trans-Atlantic shipping, throwing an immense strain on the railway system and the port of Halifax. Two days later, horrified onlookers on land saw the sinking of HMCS *Charlottetown* by U-517, with the loss of ten men, including the captain, Lt. Cdr. John Bonner.

U-517, under Paul Hartwig, appeared to have a charmed life. Before sinking the corvette, he had sent the *Donald Stewart*, the

HMCS *Sackville* at Halifax. Canada's last corvette. JBB

A U-boat under attack from the air. SAM

first Canadian ship to be sunk in the Battle of the Gulf of St. Lawrence, to the bottom and evaded attacks by HMCS *Weyburn* and a Digby aircraft whose depth charges went off prematurely. Hartwig sank three more ships, escaped numerous attacks from the sea and the air, and brought his U-boat back to base. Doenitz sent five more submarines to sink traffic in the Gulf, but they found the defences strengthened and ships and aircraft on constant patrol. After sinking the Canadian freighter *Carolus*, U-69 waited for another target.

On the night of October 14, 1942, this submarine torpedoed the ferry *Caribou* in the Cabot Strait. Its escort, HMCS *Grandmère* tried to ram the U-boat, then dropped depth charges for 90 minutes. Her captain turned to rescuing the survivors of the *Caribou*. Of the 237 passengers and crew, only 101 survived. The captain and both his sons perished, as did five mothers and ten children. As they drifted through the night on a raft, Margaret Brooke, an RCN Nursing Sister, desperately tried to keep her friend Agnes Wilkie alive. She failed, but received the OBE for her dedication.

On November 9, 1942, U-518 landed a spy near New Carlisle on the Bay of Chaleur. He carried a copy of *Mary Poppins* and some outdated Canadian currency and was quickly caught. The Allies lost 21 ships and almost 250 lives in the Battle of the Gulf, which ended in late 1942. U-boats equipped with schnorkels, a device that enabled them to recharge their batteries while submerged, tried to penetrate eastern Canadian waters in late 1944, with little success. A torpedo from U-1223 failed to sink HMCS *Magog*, although the corvette never went to sea again. On November 24/25, U-1228 sank HMCS *Shawinigan*, killing all 91 members of her crew, the RCN's greatest loss in the Gulf.

By the time of this sinking, the Allies had turned the tide in the Battle of the Atlantic. In March 1943, they lost 108 ships to submarine attacks, but sank 16 U-boats. Two months later, a wolf pack attacked convoy ON5 and lost 21 boats. Doenitz withdrew his submarines from the North Atlantic and equipped them with acoustic torpedoes that homed in on the noise of the propellors of ships.

The Allies won the Battle of the Atlantic through better co-operation between its navies and air forces and improved technology. The code breakers read German

Ops Room, Eastern Air Command, showing RCN-RCAF co-operation. Brigadier General P.D. Lloyd

Survivors of U-744 are rescued by HMCS *St. Catherines*. MCM

U-boat signals transmitted by the Enigma device. Advanced radar located submarines and aircraft from escort carriers scouted ahead of convoys. The "Black Pit" south of Greenland which could not be covered by two-engine planes vanished with the coming of VLR (Very Long Range) Liberators. These four-engine aircraft had Leigh Lights that turned night into day, illuminating U-boats on the surface. The planes then swooped down to attack them. Early in 1943, Canadian warships left the North Atlantic to operate between Britain and Gibraltar. Their crews underwent extensive training as the ships acquired better anti-submarine equipment.

In March, 1943, the RCN took over responsibility for the Northwest Atlantic, becoming a full partner with the Royal Navy and that of the United States in convoy escort. The Canadians became highly skilled in anti-submarine warfare.

But U-boats continued to sink ships.

On December 24, a torpedo from U-806 hit the minesweeper HMCS *Clayoquot* outside the entrance to Halifax Harbour. It trapped two officers in their cabin, and the survivors watched in horror as these men thrust their heads out of a scuttle, pleading for help. Then the ship sank and its depth charges exploded. On April 16, 1945, the minesweeper HMCS *Esquimault*, the 24th and last Canadian warship lost in the Second World War, sank after being torpedoed outside Halifax Harbour with the loss of 39 of her crew. A sailor on the rescue ship, HMCS *Sarnia*, recalled "hoping like hell we wouldn't get it" so near the end of the war as he pulled survivors, stiff as boards, teeth chattering, from the icy waters.

Increasingly, towards the end of the war, German submarines, captained by inexperienced officers and with poorly trained crews, proved no match for the Allied navies and air forces. Of the 40,000 sailors who served in the U-boat fleet, 28,000 died in action, and 7,000 were captured: This was the highest wartime casualty rate in any service.

Much of the success of Canadian warships depended on captains who strove to create happy ships. Some also proved to be lucky, while other ships seemed to have bad luck. The experiences of two Tribal Class destroyers illustrate the vagaries of war at sea. HMCS *Athabaskan*, commissioned in 1943, served with the Royal Navy's Home Fleet. The life and death of this warship is told in a book aptly titled *Unlucky Lady*. While under construction at Newcastle-on-Tyne, a German bomb hit the hull. On patrol between Faroes and Iceland, the warship weathered severe storms that stressed her hull and made life miserable for all on board her. On August 27, 1943, while on patrol off Spain, *Athabaskan* encountered a new peril. A Dornier aircraft released radio-controlled bombs at the ship. One went right through the destroyer without exploding, but the other killed five sailors, wounded two others, and set *Athabaskan* on fire. After a refit, Lt. Cdr. John Stubbs took command and did all he could to turn her into a happy ship. *Athabaskan* sailed with convoys to Murmansk, then patrolled around the Azores. Before D-Day, she cruised the coasts off northwest France with HMCS *Haida*, a destroyer in the same class. In a night action on April 26, 1944, the two Canadian warships set a German Fleet Torpedo Boat on fire. A few nights later they engaged two enemy destroyers off Morlaix. A torpedo smashed into *Athabaskan's* side, wrecking two guns and shattering the propulsion system, leaving her dead in the water. *Haida* pursued the German destroyer, driving it on to the rocks. At 4:28 a.m., *Athabaskan* blew up as her survivors struggled in the water. *Haida* stopped and scooped them up, while Stubbs moved among his crew, telling them to sing and to keep moving. Then this gallant officer told *Haida* to leave in case she too was torpedoed. An enemy vessel rescued some survivors, but 128 Canadian sailors died on that night, including John Stubbs.

HMCS *Haida* survived the war with the reputation of being a happy ship, and Canada's most famous one. In 1944, under Commander Harry DeWolf, she ranged up and down the English Channel, protecting the flanks of the invasion fleet on D-Day, then providing fire support for soldiers battling inland. On June 24, the destroyer raced to a spot where a RAF Liberator had depth-charged a submarine to continue the attack. The crew put pails over the sides to collect herring stunned by the blasts. While so occupied, they saw U-971 rise to the

The ships company of HMCS *Athabaskan*, with her captain, Lt. Cdr. John Stubbs in the center. He and 127 of his men did not survive the sinking of the ship on April 29, 1944. MCM

surface. *Haida's* gunners shattered its conning tower and hull. In addition to this kill, *Haida* accounted for two German destroyers, a minesweeper and 14 other enemy vessels. This happy ship, after being refitted, saw service in Korea. After she was decommissioned, the destroyer, bought by admirers, ended her days moored at Toronto, a memorial to all whom served on her – and to the men of the RCN. In Halifax, HMCS *Sackville*, Canada's last remaining corvette, restored to her wartime appearance, serves a similar purpose.

Canadian Motor Torpedo Boat flotillas operated around the French coasts and in the Mediterranean. Lt. Tom Fuller acquired the title "the Pirate of the Adriatic" while commanding an MTB assisting Tito's partisans. Service with these fast, lightly armed vessels attracted daring individuals, including Jack McClelland who later became one of Canada's leading publishers, and the artist Tony Law who told of his experiences in *White Plumes Astern*. Engaging better armed and faster German E-boats, they suffered close to 30 per cent casualties. MTB 460 struck a mine and only the gunners survived, and Law's 459 was hit by a shore battery off Cap La Havre. Life on these small boats was made more perilous by the fuel they used, highly flammable 100-octane gasoline. On February 14, 1945, the 29th MTB Flotilla lay in the inner basin of Ostend harbour with others from the Royal Navy. Water had entered the tanks of some vessels and had to be pumped out. A thin sheen of gasoline remained on the water. Then quite suddenly, it went up with a great roar in a sheet of flame. Boats blew up, throwing

HMCS *Haida*, a destroyer that became a "happy ship" and saw service in the Second World War and Korea. MCM

blazing men into the water. Five Canadian MTBs and seven from the RN were destroyed, and 26 Canadian and 35 British sailors killed.

Other Canadians were luckier, including Ronald Weyman, who commanded an LST (Landing Ship Tank) that had been converted into a communications centre. On D-Day, the ship anchored off Omaha Beach, receiving and transmitting vital information as troops landed and advanced. As Weyman wrote: "The Americans who had landed there were having a rough time and were shooting at everything, including Spitfires sent to help them." The Canadian landed on the beach on D-Day plus two to assist in acquiring German radar sets. Noting the dead in the water and the shattered landing craft, Weyman observed: "Incredibly, in the rank green grass on the beach, there were poppies in bloom." Ten days after the invasion, a Stuka released a single bomb that hit the LST. As the crew abandoned ship, corvettes swung in to pick them up. Of the ships' company of 250, only five died.

Weymans' book, *In Love and War*, is rich in anecdotes about his time in battle, told in a light hearted and modest manner. In *On the Triangle Run*, James Lamb recalls a sailor who survived the sinking of HMCS *Clayoquot* keeping up the spirits of those around him by shouting out radio news flashes: "Canadian Minesweeper Destroys German Torpedo!" Unlike the U-boat sailors, Canadians in the RCN had no illusions that they belonged to a "Master Race." Lamb notes that it was "this wry, irreverent, self-

Motor torpedo boats of the 29th MTB Flotilla at full throttle. MCM

deprecating humour, that, more than anything else, set Canadian seamen apart from our German U-boat contemporaries."

Canada's wartime sailors, dedicated volunteers and seagoing amateurs, fought and survived in the worst seas in the world and triumphed over a ruthless enemy. And many learned the wisdom of the lines of Rudyard Kiplings' poem *The Song of the Dead*:

"If blood be the price of admiralty, Lord God, we ha' paid in full!"

At the war's end, Germany still had 463 U-boats, despite all the losses. Lt. Wilfred Stokvis, while an officer on HMCS *Grandmère*, helped to rescue a seaman after the sinking of the *Caribou*. Two years later, as captain of the corvette HMCS *Barrie*, Stokvis rescued the survivors of SS *Livingston* near the site of the sinking of the ferry. Among them was the seaman he had rescued from that ship. When Germany surrendered, this officer told his men: "We can be proud of the job done. If we had lost the Battle of the Atlantic, V-E (Victory in Europe) Day would not have been ours but Germany's. Good sailing."

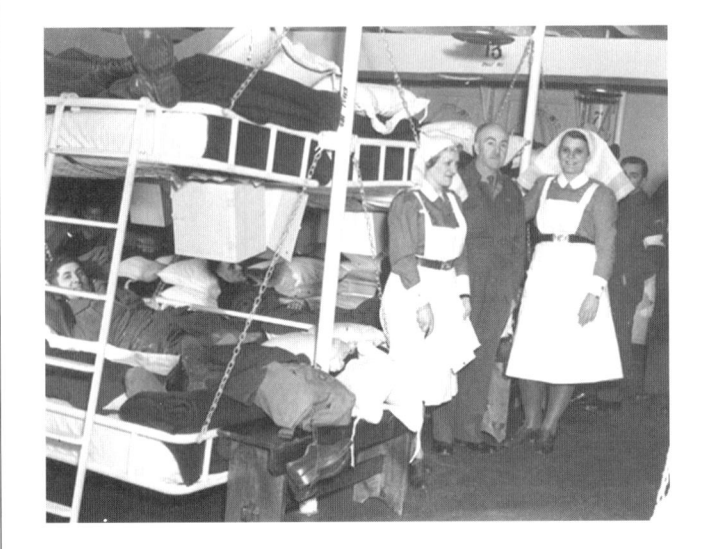

Patients and staff on No. 2 Canadian General Hospital Ship *Letitia*, docked at Liverpool, England. DND

CANADA'S MERCHANT NAVY AT WAR

"Merchant seamen virtually form the fourth arm of the fighting services, and despite their reticence to blazen abroad their exploits, we feel that in fairness to them and their next of kin, the Canadian public should be told of their work."

J. E. Michaud, Minister of Transport during the war years.

In 1939, Canada had only 38 ocean-going merchant ships, manned by about 1,450 seamen. Many others sailed in ships registered at foreign ports and in "canallers", vessels of the Great Lakes fleet that could pass through the St. Lawrence lock system. In all, 133 of these lakers became part of Canada's ocean fleet, and several of them took part in the evacuation of troops from Dunkirk. Eleven days after the last soldiers left the beaches, on June 15, 1940, U-38 torpedoed the *Erik Boye*, the first Canadian merchant ship sunk in the Battle of the Atlantic.

Canadian shipyards, almost idle at the beginning of the war, began to step up construction of new vessels. By the end of 1939, only three ships out of 410 that sailed in convoy had been lost. Convoys sailed at the speed of the slowest ship, set at 9 knots at the beginning of the war. As older vessels came into service, they assembled at Sydney to form slow convoys. Any ship that broke down and became a straggler usually fell prey to a U-boat. In the first years of the war, German battleships and armed merchant raiders, which could destroy a ship at long range, prowled the North Atlantic.

As the toll of shipping sunk by the Germans rose, a frantic race began. Could the Allies build enough ships to replace those sunk? On August 31, 1941, Convoy SC-42 left Sydney and its 64 ships and four escorts began the perilous crossing to Britain. Ten days later, 14 U-boats attacked and sank 14 ships, and 160 seamen died. To the bottom of the ocean went wheat, chemicals, explosives, timber, steel and iron ore.

Halifax became the main assembly point for traffic bound for Britain, with scores of ships waiting in Bedford Basin to join convoys. James Lamb wrote of those who served on them: "You hardly noticed them

---

The monument to the lost Canadian merchant ships on the Halifax waterfront. JBB

137

A Canadian sailor keeps watch over merchant ships, including a tanker, sailing in convoy. MCM

in Halifax...They wore no uniforms, but for all that they were the real warriors of the Battle of the Atlantic, and the youngest matelot joining an escort ship on the Triangle Run quickly learned to respect them."

Merchant seamen had a 50 per cent chance of surviving an enemy attack. Even if they took to the boats, they had no guarantee of rescue as other ships and escorts sought to escape German submarines. For their perilous work, the seaman received $75-100 a month plus a war risk bonus of $44.50.

Garfield Chinn from Newfoundland recalled the sinking of a large English ship loaded with meat from Australia. Near Freetown, Sierra Leone, a torpedo and bombs hit her: "It was some pitiful...she opened up and all that meat, the blood comin' out – the sharks started to come. The guys jumped over the side and the sharks would get 'em...Terrible."

In *Running the Gauntlet*, his oral history of the Canadian merchant navy at war, Mike Parker quotes one seaman: "There was one convoy I was in that went to England and there was 27 ships. Seven of us made it...After standing on deck and watching these ships for the last four hours getting sunk, it took quite a while to get down to relieve the other fellow below...And you know in ammunition ships you don't have a chance: you don't have a chance down below anyway."

Merchant ships waiting to join a convoy in Eastern Passage, Nova Scotia. MCM

Bernard McCluskey of Prince Edward Island went to sea at 13, and joined the *Spurt*, a Norwegian ammunition carrier, in 1941. He asked a crew member where the life jackets were. He replied: "If this thing is hit, you'll need a parachute." On the *Bristol City*, McCluskey delayed taking tea to the men in the stokehold. A few minutes later, a torpedo hit the engine room: "That was the end of that…I was supposed to be gone." After seven days in a lifeboat, the Canadian, rescued by a British corvette, went to hospital, then back to Canada: "I came home and mother near fell down…I was probably sixteen."

Only at the end of the last century did Canadian merchant seamen receive the same government benefits as those offered to other veterans of the Second World War. The Book of Remembrance of the war dead of Canada's Merchant Navy contains 1,629 names, including those of eight women. The names of other Canadians who served on Allied merchant ships remain unknown. Facing the entrance to Halifax Harbour, through which many of these men sailed on their last voyage, stands a monument inscribed:

"In Honour of the Men and Women of the Navy, Army, and Merchant Marine of Canada…Their Graves are Unknown but their Memory Shall Endure."

This Star Weekly cover of April 3, 1943 shows an imaginary scene of a German destroyer being sunk by Allied battleships. By this time, the German raiders had been driven from the North Atlantic.

The monument in Point Pleasant Park, Halifax to Canadians lost at sea who have no known grave. JBB

THE END OF THE WAR

"It was hard for the prisoners to believe they were now free. Some of them had just about given up hope..."

Brigadier Richard Malone.

With the end of the war in Europe, the attention of the Allies turned to defeating Japan. American troops had fought their way across the Pacific in a series of bloody island invasions, and the American navy and air force had crippled the Japanese at sea and destroyed most of their planes.

Canada played a minor role in the Pacific War after the disaster at Hong Kong, with some individuals and units serving with distinction. S/L Leonard Birchall of 413 Squadron became known as "The Saviour of Ceylon." On April 4, 1942, the crew of his Catalina spotted a large Japanese fleet on its way to the island now known as Sri Lanka. Birchall radioed back to his base, alerting the military there and avoiding a repeat of the attack on Pearl Harbor. Then the seaplane was shot down and three of its crew killed: The other six became prisoners of war. Birchall received the DFC and an OBE for his conduct in POW camps. Captain Bill Law of the Calgary Tanks went to Burma in 1944 to learn about jungle warfare. Captured by Japanese soldiers, he escaped as British shells fell nearby. Unarmed Dakotas of 435 and 436 Squadrons played a vital role in the Burma Campaign, dropping supplies, moving troops and evacuating the wounded. Chinese-Canadian commandos of Force 136 operated behind enemy lines in Malaya. Members of a Canadian radar detachment, lent to the Australians, served throughout South-East Asia.

With victory in Europe, the Canadian government offered its land, naval and air forces for the invasion of Japan. In the spring of 1945, the cruiser HMCS *Uganda* joined the British fleet off Okinawa. Ottawa decreed that only volunteers would serve in the Far East. The cruiser's crew voted itself out of

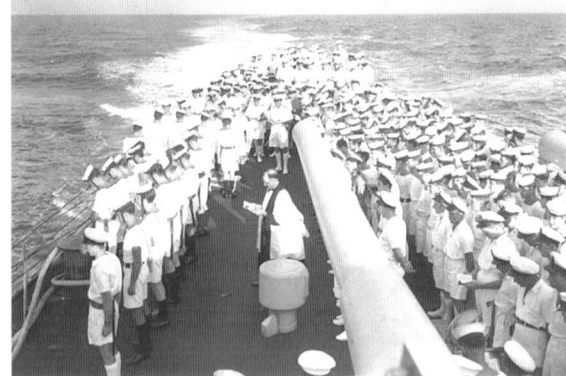

Burial service for Stoker Phillips, on HMCS *Uganda*, April 27, 1945. DND the war, and the ship headed for Canada on July 27. About 200 Canadian pilots and observers stayed in the war, attacking Japanese bases and airfields and suffering heavy losses. Lt "Hammy" Gray of the RCNVR transferred to the Fleet Air Arm, flying his Corsair fighter-bomber off the carrier HMS *Formidable*. On August 6, 1945, the first atomic bomb fell on Hiroshima. The Japanese continued to fight, and three days later, Gray led his flight against enemy vessels in Onagawa Bay on Honshu Island. Pressing on through flak, he dropped his bomb on the escort ship *Amakusa*, sinking it. Then the Canadian's plane dove into the water. For this daring attack, Gray received a posthumous VC, the only one won by the RCN during the Second World War. On the same day, Gray's friend, Lt. "Andy" Anderson crash-landed on the deck of *Formidable* and his plane fell into the sea. These two young Canadians died on the day the second atomic bomb fell on Nagasaki and the Japanese sued for peace. HMCS *Prince Robert*, which had taken the doomed Canadian contingent to Hong Kong, picked up the survivors of the battle and the camps and brought them back to Canada.

V-J Day, celebrated on August 15, 1945, ended the Second World War, with the official surrender documents being signed on September 2. Canadians in and out of uniform heaved a sigh of relief and returned to a much-changed country and world that would never be the same again after the mighty conflict of the Second World War. They settled into lives that would be marked by prosperity and pride in what a small nation had achieved in saving the world from the tyranny of Nazism and Fascism.

Top: HMCS *Uganda* bombards Sukuma Airfield on Sakishima Island, May 4, 1945. NAC
Bottom: Lt. "Hammy" Gray VC. NAC

The National War Memorial, Confederation Square, Ottawa.
Canada's Unknown Soldier, whose tomb is shown on the back cover of the book, is buried here. JBB.

THE KOREAN CONFLICT
1950-1953

*"Korea was supposed to be a 'police action'.
But it was a war in the sense that people were shooting at each other.
And people were dying…it was half war, half peace."*

Borden Brethour, Royal Canadian Ordnance Corps

At four in the morning of June 25, 1950, 90,000 North Korean troops poured south over the 38th Parallel. Led by Soviet-made T-34 tanks, they quickly pushed Korean and American troops into the south-east corner of the country around the port of Pusan. Two days later, the United Nations Security Council declared that peace had been breached and set up the UN Unified Command under General Douglas MacArthur to undertake a "police action." The Americans dispatched troops. Canada sent three Tribal class destroyers to Korean waters as the RCAF's 426 (Transport) Squadron began supply runs in support of the UN initiative.

The Korean conflict caught the Canadian government – and the nation's army – unprepared. After some dithering, the Cabinet agreed to send a contingent of volunteers to Korea as part of a multinational force. The first soldiers of the Princess Patricia's Canadian Light Infantry arrived in Korea in December 1950, at a critical point in the conflict. On September 15, with support from Canadian destroyers, MacArthur had landed troops at Inchon, near Seoul. And the American 8th Army broke out of the Pusan pocket and began to advance north.

Lt. Col. "Big Jim" Stone, commander of the Princess Pat's, refused to send his men into battle until they had trained for eight weeks. This proved to be a wise move. The Canadians soon found themselves in battle with some of the 180,000 Chinese "volunteers" who

Members of B Company, Princess Pat's move through a Korean village in February 1951. NAC

The United Nations Service Medal – Korea, awarded to all troops who served with the UN there.

had swarmed across the Yalu River in October to assist their fellow-communist North Koreans. For two years, Canadian troops attacked and defended nameless hills in Korea as battle lines moved up and down the peninsula. As Stone put it: "Korea was not a war of heroics. It was for the most part uncomfortable, fatiguing and boring." In February 1951, the Princess Pat's, part of the 27th British Commonwealth Infantry Brigade, had four men killed while attacking Hill 444. Late in April, human waves of Chinese overran Australian positions at Kapyong. Then they surged towards the Canadian lines on Hill 677, bugles blaring, whistles blowing, grenades flying, burp guns (machine pistols) chattering. In a confused night action, the men of the Princess Pat's held the line, losing ten men killed and 23 wounded. Pvt. Ken Barwise killed six Chinese and won the Military Medal. The battalion was the only Canadian unit ever to receive a United States Presidential Citation for their defence of Hill 677. Stone said of his men: "The troops attacked when ordered and defended with courage and tenacity. The war was a stupid one, but the soldiers were superb."

Canada increased its commitment to the war in May 1951 when its 25th Infantry Brigade reached Korea. Serving under American command, the Canadians moved to positions north-east of Uijongbu. Supported by tanks and a detachment of the Royal Canadian Engineers, the members of the Royal Regiment of Canada and the Royal 22è Régiment (the Van Doos) advanced towards the 38th Parallel on May 27-28. With support from the Royal Canadian Horse Artillery, the Royals attacked Chinese positions in driving rain on May 28, taking their objectives, including the village of Chail-li. The Chinese counterattacked and the Canadians withdrew to more secure defence positions after losing six dead and suffering 54 wounded.

In the summer of 1951, the war settled into a stalemate as each side dug in and fortified trenches and bunkers. Each night patrols went out to harass the enemy. By this time, the 25th Canadian Infantry Brigade had become part of the 1st Commonwealth Division, the first force of its kind in history.

The stink of death pervaded Canadian lines as troops endured the flyblown summer heat and the deep cold of Korean winters in the land of the morning calm. To relieve the monotony, the troops built a rink and played hockey at "Imjin Gardens." They shared

Maj. Gen. M. M. A. R. West, British Commander of the Commonwealth Division in Korea, invests Captain Elizabeth Pense of the Royal Canadian Army Medical Corps with the Royal Red Cross Medal. DND

their rations with poverty-stricken peasants and cared for orphaned children. Lt. Peter Worthington of the Princess Pat's set out with his men one day to ambush the Chinese. In the encounter they discovered that their weapons, except for the Sten guns, had iced up and would not fire. Then Chinese artillery opened up on them and they retreated to their own lines.

On November 22-25, 1951, the enemy attacked Hill 355 held by the Van Doos. Like Stone, their commander, Lt. Col. Jacques Dextraze, used his hard-won knowledge from the Second World War. Skillfully disposing his men, he countered the attack without difficulty. A famous photograph shows a line of tanks, led by one named "Catherine," grinding up the banks of the Imjin River in 1952. Troops from the Royal Canadian Dragoons and the Lord Strathcona's Horse fought in Korea as members of 1/2 Royal Canadian Armoured Corps Squadron under Major Jim Quinn. They played invaluable roles in attack and defence. Dextraze noted that the tank's guns were so accurate: "They could hit a dime…" He asked the tankers to fire into enemy positions a mere 40-50 metres ahead of his advancing soldiers. Dug in near Canadian lines, the tanks of the squadron protected trenches and bunkers and offered covering fire for patrols. Trooper Ron Francis recalled the two-hour watches as "the longest and loneliest times that I have ever experienced." About half the members of the 2nd Field Regiment, Royal Canadian Horse Artillery, had experience in the Second World War. It served with the Commonwealth Division, and fired close to 300,000 shells over a one-year period. The RCHA had 9 killed and 27 wounded in Korea. The 57th Independent Field Squadron rebuilt roads and bridges, including one named for a Canadian brewer who sent beer to the troops. An enemy raft floated down a river, laden with explosives to blow up a bridge. The Canadian Mobile Laundry and Bath Unit captured it. The 54th Canadian Transport Company under Major Bob Laughton drew ammunition from both American and British supply sources. As one soldier put it: "One moment the front would be perfectly quiet. The next moment all hell would break loose." So trucks stayed near the front lines, ready to supply the guns. The sporadic pattern of warfare meant that members of the Royal Canadian Army Medical Corps had to be ready to treat casualties at any time. On October 4, 1951, during an offensive, Cpl. Ernest Poole of the RCAMC, serving with the 2nd Battalion of the Royals, tended the wounded, saving the lives of at least five of them. Told to keep his head down to avoid being killed, Poole replied: "I can't help it. I have a job to do

Canadian troops en route to Korea board an RCAF North Star of 426 (Thunderbird) Squadron. DND

and I'm going to do it." Recommended for the VC, Poole received only the Distinguished Conduct Medal.

The last Canadian action in the war took place on May 2-3, 1953. A patrol of the 3rd Battalion of the Royals waited in ambush in a valley in No Man's Land, close to the Jamestown Line of UN defences. The Canadians sent up a flare. Suddenly 60 Chinese attacked, killing Lt. J.G. Maynell, the patrol leader. The Royals retreated and fell into an ambush. Lt. Doug Banton died leading a patrol to support them. Chinese infantry continued to attack as shells fell on the Canadian lines. Lt. Edgar Hollyer called down fire on his own position and the Chinese retreated. The battle ended at two in the morning, with 26 Royals dead, 27 wounded and eight captured.

The RCN sent the Tribal Class destroyers, HMCS *Iroquois*, *Athabaskan*, *Cayuga*, *Haida*, *Huron*, *Nootka*, and *Sioux* and HMCS *Crusader* to Korean waters. They blockaded the coasts, provided fire support for troop landings and evacuations, served as radar pickets for aircraft carriers and engaged in "train busting," shooting them up on lines running into enemy positions. In October 1952, the RCN suffered its only battle casualties when a shell from a North Korean shore battery hit *Iroquois*, killing three sailors and wounding ten others.

The RCAF did not participate in the air war over Korea. Canada assigned 22 fighter pilots to the 4th Fighter Interceptor Wing of the US Air Force. Flying F86 Sabre Jets, they battled MiG 15s, destroying nine of them and damaging another 12. F/L J.A. Omer Lévesque, who shot down four German planes in the Second World War, made the first Canadian kill on March 31, 1952. F/L Ernie Glover carried out 58 missions over four months in 1952, shooting down three enemy fighters and damaging three others. He received the American DFC and one from the Commonwealth.

Top: Trooper Andy Parenteau, Lord Strathcona's Horse, on a tank near ImJin River, September, 1951. DND
Bottom: Members of 2nd Battalion Princess Pat's raising the UN flag at Miryang, Korea, January, 1951. DND

S/L Andy Mackenzie, another Second World War veteran, had less luck. On December 5, 1952, he bailed out after his jet was hit by an American pilot and spent two years in captivity.

The Korean War cost Canada 516 lives, including 312 men killed in action. Max Hastings, a British historian, wrote: "…by far the most important non-American contribution was that of Canada and other nations of the British Commonwealth." The "police action" ended with the signing of an armistice and an uneasy truce on July 27, 1953. The 38th Parallel still separates the two Koreas, although there were signs of reconciliation between them in 2000. In October 1983, Sgt. John Richardson of the Princess Pat's returned to Korea and reported: "I was convinced that our fallen comrades rest in a country where their sacrifice is fully appreciated."

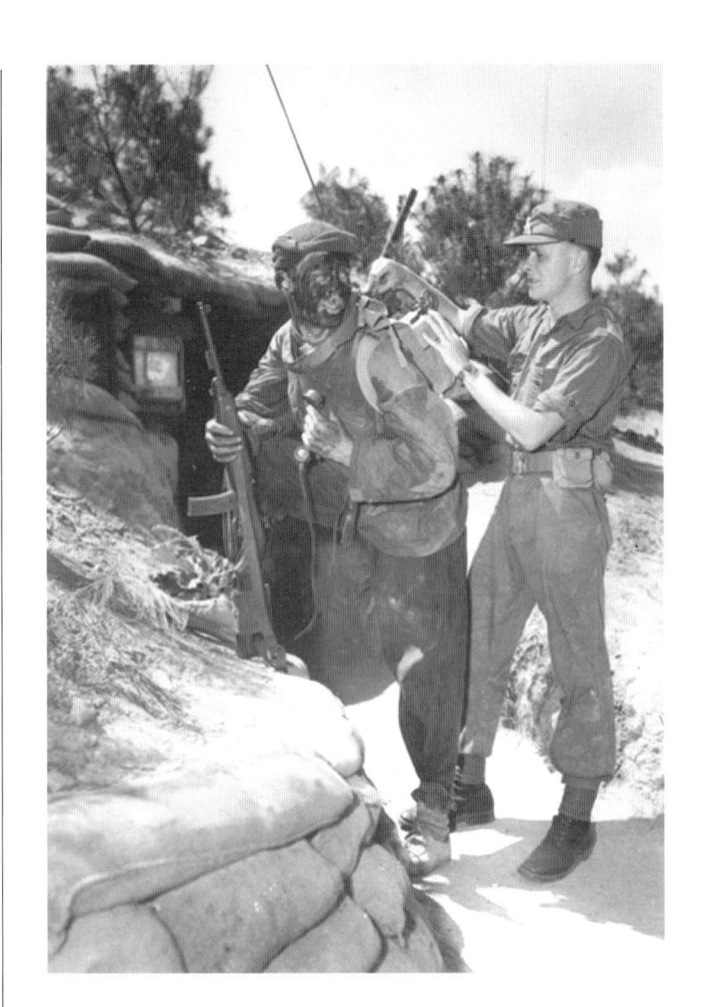

Preparing for a night patrol. Lt. Paul Ranger checks Pvt. Jean-Guy Lacroix's radio set. DND
The Canadian Korea Medal.

CANADA IN NATO & NORAD:
THE COLD WAR AND SOME HOT ONES

"Our people in the past…only achieved their maximum effort under the stress of an actual conflict."

Prime Minister Louis St. Laurent

The Cold War dominated military thinking during the last half of the Twentieth Century. In 1950, with the outbreak of the Korean conflict, the war between the western democracies and communist states became hot. In 1948, the Russian-backed communists in Czechoslovakia took over the government and tensions accelerated. The North Atlantic Treaty Organization (NATO) came into being with Canada as one of its 12 charter members on April 4, 1949. In the fall of 1951, Canadian troops moved to Europe, eventually establishing their main base as the 4th Canadian Mechanized Brigade at Lahr; Canadian air units located nearby at Baden-Sollingen.

Canadian soldiers occupied forward positions that would have been in the front lines had the Russians attacked Western Europe. Through numerous battle exercises, they honed their skills in mobile warfare. Canada's air squadrons and its ships in NATO's navy stood on guard as the organization presented a united front against any threat from the east. Things changed radically when communism collapsed and Canada's defence priorities changed.

The 4th Canadian Mechanized Brigade Group had been ordered home just as ethnic tensions in Yugoslavia exploded in 1991. Units quickly entrained to join the United Nations Protection Force

---

Soldiers of the Royal Canadian Regiment on maneouvres in Norway in 1982. DND

(UNPROFOR) seeking to keep warring groups apart as Yugoslavia disintegrated. The task of Canadian service people in the field was made more difficult by the decisions of the politicians and planners in Ottawa. In 1968, the Canadian Forces Reorganization Act created a single integrated military body, with one uniform. In 1992, as tensions accelerated in Yugoslavia, the federal government announced that all Canadians would be withdrawn from Europe.

The Canadian Army had to move swiftly from preparing for battle to peacekeeping. As they settled in at Sirac in Croatia in April 1992, the soldiers suddenly found themselves under attack. "It sounded like thunder in the distance; then seconds later we were being bombed with mortar shells," reported Cpl. Tony Carew. One man received a splinter in the buttocks and the troops began to dig themselves in as their predecessors had so often done in past wars.

In 1993, Canadian troops fought their biggest battle since Korea. But the public never heard about it because the action conflicted with the official image of our troops as "peacekeepers." Canadian paratroopers had engaged in small scale firefights in Cyprus when the Turkish troops invaded the island in 1974. The UN rules of engagement specified that those trying to keep peace under its auspices could fire back if fired upon, but could not initiate an attack.

In Yugoslavia, UN peacekeepers tried desperately to separate warring parties. But ancient hatreds made this extremely difficult – and the antagonists often had larger calibre weapons than the Canadians and other peacekeepers.

On September 9, 1993, the Croatian army attacked Serbs near the town of Medak in eastern Croatia. Caught in between the two, the Princesss Pat's suffered four casualties from mortar fire. The Canadian battalion and 500 French peacekeepers under Lt. Col. Jim Calvin tried to establish a buffer zone between Serbs and Croats. On September 15, Croat troops attacked dug-in Canadians. Sgt. Rod Dearing could not see the enemy, but directed fire at their positions. The French troops also blasted them, and the Canadians beat back several Croat attacks. Dearing's platoon killed or wounded about 30 of the attackers, for four men wounded.

Then the Croats delayed Calvin's men at a barricade while they went about looting, killing and destroying every building in the Medak Pocket. The peacekeepers pushed back the Croats and discovered evidence of ethnic cleansing. A 70-year-old woman had been shot four times, and two teenagers held by the Croats had been killed, then set on fire. Some of the soldiers began to suffer from combat fatigue, and those who carried images of atrocities back home with them fell prey to Post-Traumatic Stress Disorder.

Eighteen months after the Battle of the Medak Pocket, Calvin received the Meritorious Service Cross, and a Medal of Bravery went to WO Bill Johnston for rescuing a French peacekeeper trapped in a mine field. Eight other Canadian soldiers received Mentions in Dispatches. The United Nations recognized the participation of the Princess Pat's in the encounter with a unit citation. Lt. Gen. Gordon Reay, army chief at the time of the battle, recommended that the battalion receive a Canadian battle honour, but the request was turned down by the Department of National Defence. As Reay put it : "Maybe the department was a little gun-shy. Maybe we should have blown our own horn."

Two years earlier, however, the Governor General had approved the creation of the "Gulf and Kuwait" battle honour for those who participated in that conflict. On August 11, 1990, after Iraq's invasion of Kuwait ten days earlier, the Canadian government announced that it would send two destroyers and a supply ship to support multinational efforts against Iraq in the Persian Gulf. HMCS *Athabaskan* and *Terra Nova*, the supply ship HMCS *Protecteur*, and Sea King helicopters from 423 Squadron began to patrol the Gulf on October 1. Canadians carried out a quarter of all inspections of all ships in the region. Early in October 1990, 409 Tactical Fighter Squadron of the RCAF arrived in Doha, Qatar, and began to fly combat air patrols. In all, 26 Canadian fighters from this squadron and from 439 and 416, and a Boeing 707 for refueling them and other Allied aircraft, took part in what became known as "The Persian Excursion." Capt. "Dusty" Miller, commander of the Canadian Naval Task Force, took this phrase for the title of his book on the Gulf War.

After the conflict, Canadians did what they could to save lives. Lt. Cdr. James Hewitt gave a breezy account of his work in clearing mines in *Desert Sailor*. One day, 100 "mines" were sighted - only three turned out to be real. In March 1991, a few days after the war ended, Hewitt discovered charts of Iraqi mine fields in the Gulf while searching through a looted enemy base.

On July 11, 1991, a live-fire training exercise by an American armoured unit in Kuwait went out of control. The overheated engine of an ammunition carrier burst into flames. Howitzer shells ignited an open-air ammunition dump as American troops panicked and fled. A nearby contingent of the 1st Canadian Engineer Regiment under Capt. Fred Kaustinen, part of a UN Force monitoring the cease-fire and clearing mines, swung into action. Two soldiers donned protective clothing and plunged into the blast zone to provide an early warning post. Other Canadians set about caring for wounded and burned American troops. Then they began to remove

Top: Gas drills on HMCS *Protecteur* during the Gulf War. DND
Bottom: A member of the Van Doos with a man in Bosnia-Herzegovina who lost everything but his horse. DND

unexploded shells to safe places. The Americans lost more armoured vehicles in this disaster than during the entire Gulf War. The United States Army issued a letter of appreciation to the Canadian engineers.

Canadians went into battle again in 1999 when NATO bombed targets in Kosovo and the Federal Republic of Yugoslavia. These attacks marked the first time the Canadian Air Force had gone into combat in Europe since the end of the Second World War. It flew almost 700 sorties and dropped about 200,000 kg of high explosives. Lawyers vetted each target to determine if attacks met tests of laws on "the reasonable use of lethal force." A Canadian pilot spotted a large truck on a bridge he was about to attack. Unable to determine if it was a military or a civilian one, he radioed back to base and was ordered to return without dropping his bombs.

Rear Admiral Bruce MacLean, addressing a Parliamentary Committee on the bombing of Kosovo, had to remind its members: "…conflict is and always will be very dirty and very ugly and there will always be accidents and there will always be miscues, but that's the nature of the business."

Looking back over the past decades of Canada's military history, Canadians can take consolation from the fact that a cool-headed former fighter pilot may well have saved the world from nuclear war. Air Marshal Roy Slemon received his wings in 1924, one of the first to do so with the newly-formed RCAF. After a distinguished career,

Canadian Air Force Boeing 707 refueling CF5s. SAM

he became the first deputy commander of the North American Air Defence Command (NORAD). Set up in 1957 by the United States and Canada, this body monitors aircraft, missile and satellite movements by radar. On October 5, 1960, Air Marshal Slemon sat in the "hot seat" at NORAD headquarters at Cheyenne Mountain, Wyoming. At 3:15 p.m., Thule radar in Greenland reported 40 incoming missiles. The Canadian did not panic and order a counterstrike. Three minutes later the Thule operators reported that their radar had detected the rising sun!

Top: HMCS *Magnificent* in the company of HMCS *Haida* and *Nootka*. SAM
Bottom: A CF–18 heads for an air patrol mission over Yugoslavia. DND

CITIZENS IN SERVICE
THE RESERVES

"...a weapon infinitely more powerful, and more ready than any in the official armoury."

Farley Mowat.

In October 1939, a month after the outbreak of the Second World War, Farley Mowat, the Canadian author, tried to join the RCAF. Rejected by recruiters, he enlisted in his father's outfit, the Hastings and Prince Edward Regiment - the Hasty Ps. As an officer in the Non-Permanent Active Militia, with very little equipment, Mowat "had to be very inventive." He formed a ski platoon and devised drills and manoeuvres not known in the regular army, as he relates in his war-memoir, *And No Birds Sang*.

The success in battle that Canadians have demonstrated stems from the way in which the Militia - part-time soldiers - have learned new ways of attack and defence while drawing on the experiences of professionals. Today the Canadian Forces have four Reserves: the Militia (the Army Reserve), the Naval Reserve, the Air Reserve and the Communications Reserve. Canadian Rangers, drawn largely from Aboriginal peoples, stand guard in Canada's empty north and cadets train for life in the services.

When the CEF sailed for France in 1914, most of the officers and men came from the voluntary reserve. Since then, members of the Militia and other Reserves have played significant roles in war and peace. For many years, the Reserves welcomed women more readily than did the Regular Forces. In 1985, Mary Nangle joined 709 (Toronto) Communications Regiment, a Reserve unit,

Members of the Lincoln and Welland Regiment at Summer Militia Camp, Petawawa, July, 1950. DND

as Regular Force Advisor: "This is where I really saw men and women treated the same. The unit had radio detachments made up of all male, all female, or a mixture. It didn't matter what the mixture was, it was based on the best people for the job. It worked out very well…"

Sir Arthur Currie joined the Militia in British Columbia in 1893, while working as a teacher and real estate broker, and became one of the outstanding Allied generals of the First World War. He wrote in his diary: "Thorough preparation must lead to success. Neglect nothing." *Maclean's* magazine summed up his style: "No flashing genius but a capable administrator, cool headed and even tempered and sound in judgement…He is the last man in the world to stick to his own plan if a better one offers…he is first among equals for such is the way his staff works."

Currie exemplified the Militia style of operation – egalitarian, innovative and willing to try new approaches.

During the Second World War, the Royal Canadian Navy Volunteer Reserve, formed in 1923, attracted young men from Canada's yacht clubs who enjoyed being around boats. Many served in the small, fast ships of the navy's Coastal Forces. The "hit and run" approach of the "Champagne Navy" and the piratical life of those who served in it attracted sailors who fretted under traditional naval discipline.

Like Currie, Wilfrid Curtis rose to high rank after enlisting in the Militia. After service in the infantry in the First World War, he became a fighter pilot in the Royal Naval Air Service. After the war, while running his own insurance firm, Curtis formed a squadron of the Non-Permanent Active Air Force. During the Second World War, he served as Air Officer Commanding the RCAF in London, and pressed for more autonomy for the service. Curtis ended his military career in 1953 as Chief of the Air Staff.

The spirit that motivates the members of today's reserves becomes apparent when you talk with them. "Comradeship", is how Lt. Colin Smith of the West Novas – his grandfather's regiment – sums it up. "When you're sharing a trench with someone, you talk about everything and become really close," adds Sgt. Andrew Pendelbury of the Princess Louise Fusiliers.

Sgt. Mary Nangle comes from a military family. She's the only member who was not a cadet or a member of the Reserves before entering the regular forces. Her father was the Regimental Sergeant Major of the 51st Service Battalion in Montreal who became its honorary Lt. Col. after he retired. Two brothers and a sister joined the unit while their father served as RSM, and another brother went straight from cadets into the

---

Canadian Forces Rangers, Grise Fiord, Ellesmere Island. DND

army. The six members of the family in the services have spent time in postings across Canada, the United States, Germany, New Zealand, Egypt, Israel, Cyprus, Namibia, Bosnia-Herzegovina, Croatia, and Kosovo and have received 11 medals for peacekeeping.

In the Reserves, young men and women discover qualities in themselves and others that they never before recognized. As Smith puts it: "You develop competence in so many aspects of life, acquiring skills, determining your leadership potential."

Reserve members on peacekeeping missions who return to civilian life, rather than to the comradeships of regiments, often have trouble adjusting to normality in Canada. Most cannot forget the horrors they have seen. Others pass on what they have learned to others. Pendelbury teaches members of his unit to dig trenches and mediate disputes: "I've been in trenches and I've been shot at. You learn to be confident, to know when to use your mouth and when to use the radio." And he recalls one incident that has stayed with him: "An old woman in Croatia rose at 4:30 a.m. every morning and brought us coffee when we finished our time in the line. When we moved out and the troops of another nation moved in, she stood there, silent, watching us leave. And she was crying."

Cadets work on the Trans Canada Trail in 1999. DND

The PEACEFUL USES OF CANADA'S ARMED FORCES

"The grim fact is that we prepare for war like precocious giants and for peace like retarded pygmies."

Lester B. Pearson, Acceptance Speech, Nobel Peace Prize, Oslo, Norway, December 10, 1957.

The years after the Korean conflict spawned a new acronym – PUMF. It stands for "Peaceful Uses of Military Forces." While the armed forces of the western democracies stood on guard against communism, governments found new roles for the men and women in their armies, navies and air forces. Four years before the outbreak of the First World War, the American philosopher William James wrote about a problem that bedevils our own time. In his essay, "The Moral Equivalent of War," he described war as "the strong life." It brings to the fore many desirable human qualities – dedication to ideals, selflessness, comradeship – as well as offering endless opportunities for the exercise of evil. James saw the central issue of his time as "one of turning the individual and collective heroism and sacrifice demanded by war into more constructive channels."

Through a wide range of activities, Canada's service men and women are showing how this can be done. They have become giants in providing aid to the civil power in times of crisis, on special missions in Canada, and especially in peacekeeping.

One of the enduring images in 1990 was of a young Canadian soldier, Pvt. Patrick Cloutier, standing almost nose to nose with a "Mohawk warrior" during the Oka crisis. A dispute between First Nations people and local residents turned violent. Barricades went up, and armed, masked men confronted members of the Sûreté du Québec. Police rushed the barricades and one officer died in the

An Army post during the Oka crisis, September 1990. DND

The "Flying Banana," a Labrador helicopter used for rescue work. SAM

gunfight. On August 17, the Québec government asked the Canadian Forces to replace provincial police and dismantle the barricades. The soldiers did so with the minimum of fuss and the crisis ended. Almost 20 years earlier, on October 15, 1971, the Quebec government requested Ottawa to send in soldiers during the FLQ crisis to "help the police protect the public and public buildings." A small number of extremists kidnapped a British trade official and the Québec Labour Minister, Pierre Laporte. Prime Minister Pierre Trudeau invoked the War Measures Act to deal with an "apprehended insurrection", and armed soldiers guarded the houses of key politicians and others in Ottawa.

Members of Canada's Armed Forces enjoyed a more rewarding time in Québec when 16,000 of them took part in what was claimed to be their biggest combined operation since the Second World War – providing security at the Montreal Olympics in 1971. In April of that year several hundred Canadian soldiers entered Kingston penitentiary after prisoners seized six hostages. This incident ended peacefully.

The special missions carried out by members of the Canada's Armed Forces range from ceremonial parades to search and rescue efforts that have saved countless lives. In Canada's North, service men and women have built airfields – and recovered remnants of Cosmos 954, the nuclear-powered Russian satellite that shattered in Canadian air space in January 1978.

Providing relief and assistance in times of emergency has proved rewarding to members of the services. They rescued stranded people during the great Winnipeg Flood in 1950 – and provided help to the people of the Netherlands in 1954 when their land flooded. Canadian soldiers restored services to stricken areas in Ontario and Québec after the Great Ice Storm of 1998 – and later helped to unblock the streets of Toronto after a massive snowstorm paralyzed that city.

RCAF Hercules delivered 10 per cent of the oil needs of Zambia after independent Rhodesia (now Zimbabwe) cut off supplies to the African nation in the mid-Sixties. After a cyclone killed more than 200,000 people in April 1971, in East Pakistan (now Bangladesh), an Air Force Boeing 707 and four Yukons flew 13 missions, delivering 200, 000 kg of medicine, blankets, tents, and food. In the previous year, Air Force planes flew in supplies and evacuated survivors after an earthquake in Peru. Service personnel assisted Jamaicans to clean up the mess after a hurricane hit the island in 1988. In 1989, 12 Canadian military engineers flew to Peshawar in Pakistan to train Afghans to deal with the millions of mines strewn throughout their battered land. Capt. Karen Durnford, second-in-command of the unit, noted: "The reason I wanted to be an engineer was to go into the field." Like so many of her comrades, she relished the challenge of doing new things in a strange land.

The participation of the military in "Operation Hazen," part of Canadas' contribution to the International Geophysical Year in 1957-58, exemplified the relaxed and cheerful way in which its members accepted unusual assignments. They tackled the problems of supporting the

Main photo – The C–119, Flying Boxcar, took freight and passengers all over the world. SAM
Clockwise from top right: A soldier guards a building at Canadian Forces Base Valcartier, during the October Crisis in 1970. DND M/Cpl. Mike Claridge and Cpl. Dave Marcotuilio remove a downed tower with a Badger armoured vehicle during Operation Recuperation. This initiative aided victims of the January 1998 ice storm in Eastern Ontario and Western Quebec. DND Leading Seaman Tony Lopuck, a naval reservist with HMCS *Chippawa* in Winnipeg, helps a soldier shoring up a dike during the 1997 flood. DND Yukon delivering relief supplies in East Pakistan. SAM
Canadian sappers shore up a road in Holland in 1954. DND

"boffins" (scientists) with energy and enthusiasm, while wondering why such people would choose to spend their summers on icecaps in Northern Ellesmere Island. In late April 1957, Sgt. Dave Engel of the Royal Canadian Engineers landed in the first C-119 that touched down on frozen Lake Hazen. A ski-wheel DC-3, piloted by W/C J.G. Showler had already checked out the suitability of the lake as a landing site. Engel had not volunteered for the expedition, and no one knew if the lake ice could sustain a heavily-laden "Flying Boxcar." But it did, and in –30C weather, Engel bulldozed a one thousand metre long landing strip for the expedition's cargo planes and DC-3. His hard work, mechanical knowledge and incredible cheerfulness endeared the sergeant to the scientists and he returned in the spring of 1958 to put in the landing strip, accompanied by Sgt. J.E. Robertson of the Royal Canadian Signals who ensured that the expedition's radio equipment functioned properly.

During the summer of 1958, the RCAF again brought in supplies and lent a DC-3 piloted by F/L Merv Utas to assist the scientific research by taking parties around northern Ellesmere Island. Utas and his crew set up an unofficial "Arctic Air Command" at the base camp on Lake Hazen, with a rather rude motto. And they appointed Lt. Cdr. Jim Croal of the RCN, who had helped to guide US Coast Guard supply vessels into Chandler Fiord on the Eastern side of Ellesmere Island, "Swiss Admiral." Landings and take-offs by DC-3s had never been attempted on glacial ice at such high latitudes and at high elevations. Merv Utas and his crew learned to do them by doing them, developing techniques for lifting the plane off glaciers with the help of JATO (Jet Assisted Take Off) pods. Utas and his crew landed near Ward Hunt Island on the extreme northern coast of Canada, liberated cans of alcohol left there by Robert Peary, the American explorer who camped there in 1906, and created a powerful cocktail christened "Peary's Peril."

Members of Canada's Armed Forces have developed special skills in rescuing people from perilous situations on land and sea. Just after Christmas 1980, a couple and their two children faced death as the flood waters of the Cheakmus River rose around their cabin, 80 kms north of Vancouver. A Search and Rescue helicopter took off from Squamish airport in darkness, high winds and driving rain. Piloted by Major Keith Gathercole, it hovered above a house showing a light in the flooded river valley. SAR (Search and Rescue) Tech Steve Gledhill, dangled perilously above the house and then crashed on to its roof. Hauled up by the chopper crew, he descended again and found people crouched in the house. "They couldn't get out and in all probability they would have died there. Thank God we saw their light – and it was only a candle", Gathercole recalled. The couple were not the family that he and his crew had set out to save. By the time they found their home, it had begun to crumble and the helicopter's fuel was running low. SAR Tech Craig Seaver dropped into the raging waters behind the house, and began the rescue by taking up the mother and her baby on the first cable-hoist. Then Gledhill went down to pick up the father and the three-year-old son. Both refused to be rescued. Gledhill grabbed the child and lifted him to safety, kicking and screaming. Then he went back for the father.

In April 1983, Craig Seaver, who had been awarded the Star of Courage, took part in the rescue of three survivors of a small plane. It had crashed on Chehalis Mountain, 100 kms east of Vancouver. Descending in a large rescue net with George Makowski, another SAR Tech, Seaver jumped with him on to a snow slope. Then the two men made their way to the crash site. Soon the survivors, given emergency medical aid, were on their way to safety. On the following day, at the request of the pilot's wife, Seaver and Arnie Macauley recovered the man's body. The three SAR Techs received the Medal of Bravery in 1986 for "conspicuous courage in circumstances of great peril." In November 1996, SAR Techs Keith Mitchell and Bryan Pierce won the Cross of Valour. A Danish trawler northeast of Labrador reported that Joshua Alookie, a crew member, had taken ill. With no handy ports or landing places nearby, the decision was taken to parachute Mitchell and Pierce into the icy waters near the trawler as the only way to save the sick man's life. The two men, recovered with great difficulty by the trawler crew, treated Alookie and saw him begin to recover.

Canada's military planes and ships no longer scour the country's coasts for signs of enemy submarines. Now they carry out endless patrols, often in foul weather, searching for signs of drug smuggling, illegal fishing in Canadian waters, and ocean pollution. And, every so often, they have to rescue those in peril on the sea. On December 4, 1983, the Search and Rescue Centre in Halifax received a "Mayday" call from the

A Sea King helicopter lands on the deck of one of Canada's warships. SAM

bulk carrier, *Ho Ming 5*. Its cargo had shifted in heavy seas off Newfoundland's Grand Banks. HMCS *Iroquois*, a helicopter destroyer on fisheries patrol, sped toward the *Ho Ming 5* as an Aurora from Greenwood's 415 Maritime Patrol Squadron circled the battered vessel. With seas breaking over her deck, *Iroquois* sent its Sea King helicopter aloft. In the stormy seas and darkness of night it proved impossible to lift the crew off the deck of the *Ho Ming 5*. Just before dawn, the captain decided to abandon ship as its list worsened. Two Zodiacs and the ship's helicopter rescued the carrier's 20 Korean crew members. They left the rescue ship with *Iroquois* badges pinned or sewn to their clothes and several hundred dollars donated by the Canadian sailors.

In 1998, Canadian service personnel had the grisly task of recovering human remains from the waters off Peggy's Cove after the crash of Swissair Flight 111.

And in peacekeeping in troubled countries throughout the world, the men and women of Canada's Armed Forces often confront danger and uncertainty. They have learned how to cope with all kinds of threats, ranging from poisonous snakes to drunken warlords.

Peacekeeping offers the same sorts of tensions as service in wartime - long periods of monotony interspersed with times of sheer terror. The idea of international peacekeeping arose in 1931 when the League of Nations, the predecessor of the United Nations (UN), drafted a "Convention to Improve the Means of Preventing War." But the League lacked the will and the resources to create a peacekeeping force. In theory, the concept of peacekeeping is simple. You place a neutral, armed body between warring parties to stop them fighting and let the diplomats on each side work out ways of bringing about peaceful resolutions to conflict. In practice, peacekeeping is difficult, with those in the middle coming under fire from both sides while ancient hatreds and tensions make any resolution of conflicting demands impossible. In 1954, Lt. Gen. E.L.M. Burns became the Chief of Staff of the United Nations Truce Supervisory Team (UNTSO), the first of these initiatives by the world body. It assigned soldiers, including some Canadians, to patrol the troubled border between the state of Israel and its Arab neighbours. Other Canadians served with the International Control Commission in Vietnam, Laos and Cambodia, beginning in 1954. But the UN failed to stop wars breaking out in the Middle East and Indo-China.

Something more innovative was needed to prevent future conflict and to separate enemies bent on annihilating each other. The opportunity for this new approach to peacekeeping came in 1956 when Britain, France and Israel invaded Egypt after President Nasser nationalized the Suez Canal. Canada refused to support Britain, and the United States condemned the invasion. Canada took the lead in drafting a UN resolution to create an emergency international force "to secure and supervise cessation of hostilities." Lester B. Pearson, Canada's Minister of External Affairs, played a leading role in bringing the UN force into being and easing the invaders out of Egypt. He received the Nobel Peace Prize in 1957 for his efforts, and Canada became the first UN member to earmark a military unit for peacekeeping duties.

Top: Divers from Fleet Diving Unit (Atlantic) and (Pacific) recover remains from Swiss Air Flight 111 which crashed on September 2nd, 1998. DND
Middle: An RCAF Caribou aircraft serving with the UN. SAM
Bottom: Lt. Gen. E.L.M. Burns, Chief of Staff of the United Nations Truce Supervisory Team (UNTSO). DND

An Argus Maritime Patrol Aircraft equipped with anti-submarine warfare devices overflies a ship. SAM

HMCS *Magnificent* with Avengers on flight deck. In 1957 "Maggie" took the first Canadian unit to serve with UNEF to Egypt. SAM

Since 1947, over 100,000 Canadian service men and women have undertaken peacekeeping duties under UN auspices, about a third of them in Cyprus. Most Canadians support these efforts and the nation has developed an international reputation in peacekeeping. When Canadian troops arrived in the Sinai peninsula in 1973 after the end of the Yom Kippur War, the Finnish commander of the UN Emergency Force, Lt. Gen. Ensio Siilasvuo said: "I can't express how relieved I was when I heard the Canadians were coming."

Dr. Desmond Morton, Canada's leading military historian, writes of peacekeeping: "It used to be a matter of invitation and relatively benign. That is not the case of Peacekeeping à la Somalia, Bosnia, Haiti and (to a degree) Cambodia, where nasty people on all sides want you out."

Unfortunately, media coverage of the peacekeeping too often focuses on isolated incidents of behaviour by a few deviant individuals rather than showing how the majority of service personnel have adapted and endured in new kinds of "No Man's Land."

On Cyprus, Canadian soldiers patrolled the Green Line separating Greeks and Turks in 1964. Ten years later, they had front row seats when the Turks invaded the island. Caught in the crossfire between the two armies, Canadian soldiers rescued civilians and suffered casualties while doing so. In 1960, a contingent of 280 signallers under Capt. John Pariseau arrived in war-torn Congo on a UN mission. They were taken into custody, stripped, beaten with rifles and threatened with death.

As a young officer, John Gardam served on the first Canadian mission in Egypt in 1956. As he put it: "You can't do peacekeeping without getting to know people on the ground and earning their respect." Mutual aid marked relationships with the Bedouin. Canadians provided first aid for their children, shared their water and retrieved goats that wandered into minefields. The Bedouin warned patrols about buried mines. Gardam recalled a courageous woman who spent the night by the body of a peacekeeper killed in a mine field to ward off prowling dogs.

As in war, death can come with terrible suddenness to Canadians keeping the peace in distant lands. A special exhibit in the Canadian War Museum in Ottawa lists the names of over 100 Canadian service people who have died on UN missions. On September 27, 1957 Sgt. Ivan Stark's jeep hit a mine and he became the sixth Canadian peacekeeper to die. In May 2000, a landmine training centre at Canadian Forces Base Kingston was named after Stark.

More than 28,000 Canadians have served as peacekeepers in the Middle East, and 48 have died there. Experience here, however, offered little direction to Canadian service personnel sent to Croatia and Bosnia. Many of them had a hard time coping with life in a ruined land where civil society had fallen apart and ancient hatreds led to vicious killings of innocent people. An Army chaplain outlined some of the stresses the troops faced: "It was manageable. It was hard. We came face to face relatively early in our tour with the reality that our own soldiers are paying for this peace with their lives. And that was brought home very early

On watch in Cyprus. Royal Canadian Dragoons on Egyptian – Israeli border. Canadian armoured cars on patrol in the Congo. Canadian Forces Griffon helicopter flies over Albanian – Kosovar protestors in Mitrovica. DND

to us and it continued to follow us throughout our tour."

Canadian peacekeepers drove their vehicles into areas in Croatia under attack by Serbs in the hope that this would stop the shooting, continuing the tradition of boldness and discipline that marks Canada's record in war: "[This] was totally against what we were supposed to be doing, but they did it because their concern was to protect life." Peacekeepers wrote home for blankets, pens and paper for people who had lost everything, and they often had to recover the bodies of victims of ethnic cleansing. One soldier recalled finding a terrified old man wandering around a town. He handed him over to two local residents. They shot him. When the Canadian said he would call the police, the two men calmly showed him their badges: "We are the police."

Canadians became skilled in this new kind of peacekeeping. In February 2000, Canadians stood with other NATO troops stopping rioters from storming a bridge in Kosovo Mitrovica. Their commander, Colonel Ian Fenton, noted: "I'm always concerned because we are in a country filled with hate, in an area where people use violence as a means to settle any dispute or to show their displeasure, but our people are well prepared. They are well trained and they are well protected. They are doing a task they know is important."

In wartime, everyone soldiers on, hoping they won't get theirs, knowing that sooner or later, the conflict will end. In peacekeeping in places like the former Yugoslavia, the horror goes on endlessly, rooted in centuries of hatred between different peoples. Over time, this wears down even the most idealistic individual.

Seeing the divisions between people in strife-torn countries, members of the military reflect on how their experiences changed their view of Canada. As Cpl. Lee Riswold put it: "I figure we can get along with just about anybody. Service with the UN in Cambodia and Haiti sure makes you appreciate life in Canada." While helping with logistics in 1993 during a UN sponsored election in Cambodia, Riswold put up perimeter wire: "One of the team slid down a slope and landed on a mine. Fortunately if was a dud." Haiti offered other challenges. Riswold recalled the heat and the piles of garbage in the streets - and the dangerous traffic: "It's kind of tense. Friends went out to supper and were hit by a truck. Two of them had to be evacuated back to Canada.

Captain John McLearn of the Royal Canadian Regiment discovered at three o'clock one afternoon in January 1992, that he had to be ready to fly to El Salvador on the following day. The government and guerillas had finally stopped fighting and signed a peace treaty on December 16, 1991. Spanish-speaking countries had no troops to spare, so McLearn joined 53 other Canadian officers checking and verifying the numbers and weapons of the former warring parties. McLearn stated: "As a professional soldier, I never have a reason for refusing an assignment offered to me." With a Spanish paratrooper, he became the sole authority in and around the town of Los Marias. The area had been fought over for 12 years, and the only support for McLearn and his colleague lay 21 km away:

"We were everything. We didn't sleep terribly much. We had to ensure that a nearby guerilla brigade stayed in its area of concentration." The peacekeepers learned that this group was moving around, so they set out one night to intercept them. Hearing sounds, they switched on the high beams of their vehicle. McLearn shouted: "Hi guys! What are you doing?" The guerillas recognized the only Canadian voice in the region, and the two UN officers later convinced their leader to stop the patrols. McLearn identified the Canadian style of peacekeeping: "We have a fine reputation for getting things squared away without too much fuss and bother. We also keep a firm grip on our own operations, and we are always at the ready."

In 1998, the peacekeeping centre at Cornwallis, Nova Scotia, named after Lester B. Pearson, published *Eyewitnesses to Peace*, a collection of letters compiled by Jane Snailham. They highlight comradeship ("we lost two more of our guys...it's as if a part of every one of us over here has died"), tenacity("but we are Canadians and we will overcome"), fatalism ("God chooses the ones he wants"), making the best of conditions ("this place is seriously screwed up"), compassion ("we can only hope the future holds something promising for these poor people who have to endure so much"), and personal reward ("we wouldn't trade this mission for anything in the world. It's exactly the kind of fulfilling, personally rewarding mission we dream of.")

In peacekeeping, as in war, members of Canada's Armed Forces have few illusions about what they can achieve, even with their best efforts. From somewhere in Rwanda, a soldier wrote: "The system is not working well - we are meant to make it better. It should be easy to make it better, as it is so bad. I do not think it will be possible to get it right."

Jim Davis served as a peacekeeper in Croatia, Bosnia and Rwanda and told of his army life in *The Sharp End: A Canadian Soldier's Story*. After a series of dead-end jobs, Davis became a member of the Royal Canadian Regiment in 1985 and revelled in his role: "It was a great time to be a young soldier." Before setting out on a UN assignment in the former Yugoslavia, Davis wrote: "For myself, I am calm. I feel lucky to be part of this adventure. Whatever lies ahead, I know I am surrounded by twenty of the best men I ever met."

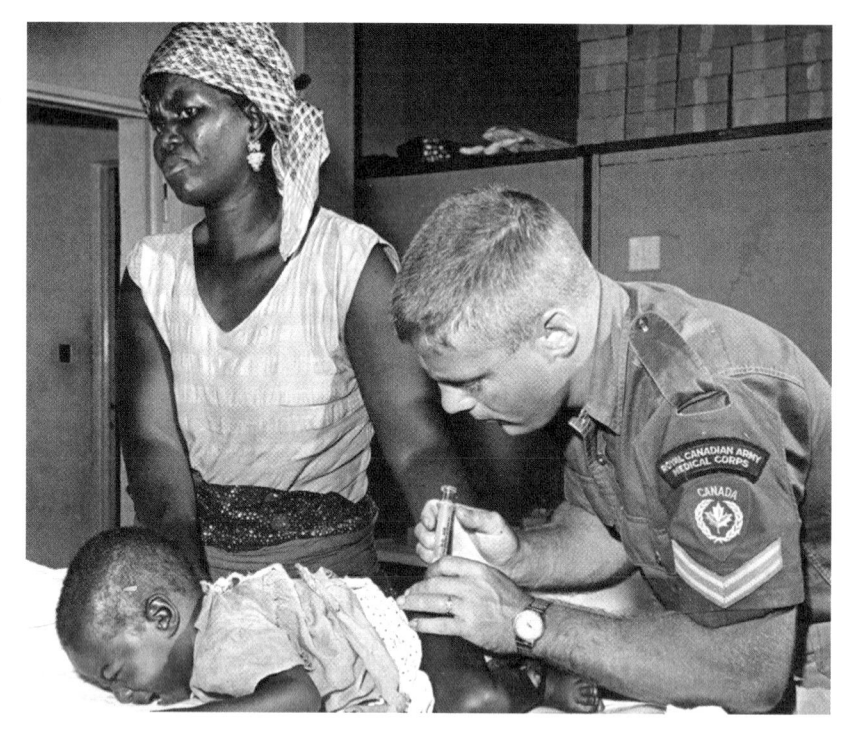

A Canadian medic administers penicillin to a Congolese baby. DND

Top: Cougars in a Bosnian winter. Cpl. Mark Bergeron
Middle: The new Canadian reconnaissance vehicle, the Coyote in Kosovo, April 1999. Photo: MCpl. John Clevett
Bottom: Bison in Bosnia, 7 September, 2000. Photo: MCpl. Ken Allen

Davis and his comrades came under fire in Croatia - to their surprise: "We were Canadians." The Canadians soon discovered how inadequate their vehicles and equipment were for the assigned tasks. Like any good soldier, Davis scrounged what he could to replace the inferior official issue. He found Sarajevo "surreal." Escorting a UN official, Davis noticed an historical marker on a bridge – the spot where Gavrilo Princip shot Archduke Ferdinand in June 1914, the act that triggered the First World War.

In June 1994, Davis transferred to the Airborne Regiment and spent three months in Mareru, Rwanda, guarding a Canadian hospital. Members of the regiment undertook many acts of kindness for the local people, caring for their sick and injured, giving their dead a decent burial. When Airborne soldiers relieved a French Foreign Legion outpost in a jungle village, they discovered a large pit filled with dead and dying prisoners. The French dealt with anyone considered to be a criminal by throwing the person into the pit and leaving him to die. The Canadians separated the living from the dead and gave them medical attention.

Davis sums up his life in the military in words that resonate through all in it: "I had the opportunity to see things and be part of some of the great events of our time…Best of all, I got a chance to meet and work with the best people this country will ever produce. The bonds of friendship, the camaraderie, the absolute trust…was without equal."

Major-General Raymond Crabbe, who served as Deputy Commander of the United Nations Protection Force (UNPROFOR) in the former Yugoslavia in 1994–95 saw many examples of brutal and ruthless behaviour: "Canadians have a terrible innocence about what happens in places like Bosnia when civil order breaks down.

Top: An Air Transport Group Hercules delivers relief supplies. DND
Bottom: Soldiers of the Van Doos on a landing craft approach the beach at Suai, East Timor. HMAS *Tobruk* in background. DND

In such situations, it's very hard to tell the good from the bad. We are impartial, well trained and have no bias towards any faction. We stay in the middle - in true Canadian fashion. We're credible as a nation and as a military presence."

As in the two world wars, in South Africa and Korea, Canadians are often asked to take on the hardest tasks by UN commanders. As in wartime, they have not been found wanting. Crabbe says of the future of peacekeeping, a moral equivalent of war that William James could never have envisaged: "The whole process has become much more complex, difficult and dangerous. Future situations…will be much more fluid. No hard and fast battle lines. No more simply sitting in OPs (Observation Posts). We will be working closely with civilian organizations, serving as protective extensions of humanitarian efforts."

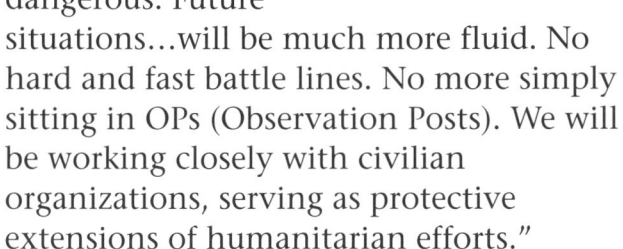

In March 2000, Camp Maple Leaf in Zumalia, East Timor, closed its doors. Canadians served there for six months with a UN force, keeping the peace after the new nation gained independence from Indonesia. Two platoons returned from a patrol to take part in the farewell ceremonies. They had been in the jungle, trying to flush out militia from West Timor who threatened the fragile peace on the island. The militia evaded them, but the Canadians made the region safer as local people put their lives together in a land ravaged by war.

East Timor is remote from South Africa. Flushing out dangerous men in its jungle is a far cry from chasing Boers on the veldt. However, members of the Canadian military have demonstrated their skills in both areas. In a time of rapid change, the record of Canada's Armed Forces has shown continuity and coherence based on values such as comradeship, initiative, unit pride, discipline - and raw courage. These qualities are as valuable in building a civil society as they are in creating a strong military force. Thus a study of Canada's military history can yield lessons for all those seeking to make this country a better and more dynamic nation.

Top: HMCS *Protecteur* in Darwin, Australia before sailing to East Timor. DND
Bottom: A Sea King helicopter delivers humanitarian aid in Suai, East Timor. DND

Thomas Riley (right) of Scarborough, ON and his son M/Cpl Ron Riley of Canadian Forces Base, Kingston, ON, at the Groessbeek Canadian War Cemetery near Nijmegen, in the Netherlands. Mr. Riley returned to the place where he was wounded during the Second World War. Father and son participated in the annual four–day, 160 km Nijmegen March. This photo was taken on July 15, 2000. DND

FURTHER READING

This book has done no more than skim the surface of Canada's long and impressive record of service in war and peacekeeping. It has drawn on an extensive range of sources from interviews with veterans to official histories. Others have documented their experiences in Canada's Armed Forces and this country has a number of distinguished military historians and writers who have told stories of our service men and women and provided a context for them.

Two prominent historians who served in the Canadian Army, Gerald Nicholson and Charles Stacey, wrote official histories and other books on its performance in the First and Second World wars. Nicholson also wrote a history of Canada's Nursing Sisters.

A new generation of Canadian historians has built on the tradition of these pioneers and produced readable and reliable books on this country's military history. Desmond Morton's book *A Military History of Canada*, is a standard, short work updated regularly. The title of Morton's *When Your Number 's Up* reflects the fatalism of the First World War soldiers he describes.

With J.L. Granatstein, Morton wrote *Marching to Armageddon* on that war, and *A Nation Forged in Fire* on the Canadian experience in the Second World War. With David Bercuson, Granatstein wrote a companion volume to these two books: *War and Peacekeeping* covers Canada's "limited wars" from South Africa to the Gulf.

The history of the RCAF is covered in three massive tomes: *Canadian Airmen and the First World War* by S.F. Wise, *The Creation of a National Air Force* by W.A.B. Douglas and *The Crucible of War* 1939-1945, by Brereton Greenhous, Stephen J. Harris, William C. Johnston and William G.P. Rawling.

Joseph Schull's *The Far Distant Ships* tells the story of the RCN in the Second World War. Tony German's *The Sea is at Our Gates* and Marc Milner's *Canada's Navy: The First Century* cover the history of the RCN.

Arthur Bishop, son of Billy Bishop, served as a Spitfire pilot in the Second World War. He has written three books of short biographies of Canadians at war: *Courage in the Air*, *Courage on the Battlefield*, and *Courage at Sea*. His book, *Our Bravest and Our Best*, tells the stories of Canada's VC winners. Francis Blatherwick's *1000 Brave Canadians* gives details of Canadian Gallantry Awards from 1854 to 1989. John Marteinson's *We Stand on Guard* traces Canada's military roots from 1627 to current peacekeeping efforts and contains hundreds of illustrations.

Veterans' Affairs Canada has issued several short, bilingual accounts of Canada's military history. A series entitled *Valour Remembered* covers the First and Second World wars and the Korean Conflict. Other publications cover The Battle of the Atlantic, The Battle of the Gulf of St. Lawrence, Canada's Merchant Navy at war (*Valour at Sea*), John McCrae, and Remembrance Day. *Native Soldiers: Foreign Battlefields* covers the history of the contributions to the military achievements of Canada by First Nations' people.

Many Canadian military units have issued their own histories or had books written about them. *Battle Royal* by D.J. Goodspeed covers the history of the Royal Regiment of Canada from 1862 to 1962. *Airborne* by Brian Nolan tells the story of the 1st Canadian Parachute Battalion in the Second World War. *The Brigade*, by Terry Copp (who has written extensively on the Second World War), deals with the Fifth Canadian Infantry Brigade between 1939 and 1945. *Courage Remembered* by G. Kingsley Wood and Edward Gibson documents the work of the Commonwealth War Graves Commission and gives the location of the cemeteries where so many Canadians lie buried. Ken Bell's *The Way We Were* contains photographs of battlefields in north-west Europe – and what they looked like in recent years.

David Bercuson and J.L. Granatstein's *Dictionary of Canadian Military History* is an invaluable work, as is *The Oxford Companion to the Second World War*, edited by I.C.B. Dear. *Canadian Militaria: Directory and Sourcebook*, produced by Service Publications (PO Box 33071, Ottawa, ON, K2C 3Y9) contains lists of associations, collectors' groups, cyber sites, museums, publishers, re-enactment societies, research resources and veterans' groups. *Canadian Military History*, issued by Wilfrid Laurier University (Waterloo, ON, N2L 3C5) contains scholarly papers and first hand accounts by veterans. Its book review supplement, edited by Jonathan Vance, provides up-to-date coverage of what is appearing in the field in Canada and elsewhere.

Some veterans have published their own memoirs and helped others to tell their stories. Ian Maxwell set up Little Daisy Press on Tancook Island, Nova Scotia, and produced two collections of Second World War memoirs – *This Was My War, And It Was My War Too*. General Store Publishing House (1 Main Street, Burnstown, ON K0J 1G0) has issued a number of accounts of wartime experiences, many of them compiled by John Gardam, one of Canada's first peacekeepers. One book contains stories from those who served in Korea. The history of that conflict is told in John Melady's *Korea: Canada's Forgotten War*, the best account of Canada's participation in the "police action." This author has also written *Heartbreak and Heroism: Canadian Search and Rescue Stories*. Mike Parker's *Running the Gauntlet* provides an oral history of Canadian Merchant Seamen in the Second World War.

Like those who saw combat, many Europeans and others who survived blitzes, invasions and war as civilians and came to Canada after the Second World War do not talk about their experiences. And it is impossible to understand why Canadians served, suffered and died in distant lands without some knowledge of the history of these places and of the Twentieth Century. In *Rites of Spring: The Great War and the Birth of the Modern Age*, Modris Eksteins, born in Latvia in 1943 and now a Canadian professor of history, describes how events in Europe brought about two world wars. *Walking Since Daybreak* blends his personal experiences with an overview of historical events to tell: "A story of Eastern Europe, World War II, and the Heart of Our Century."

The Author

Jim Lotz grew up in Liverpool, England and in rural Scotland. His father served with the Liverpool Scottish and the King's African Rifles in the First World War, but seldom spoke about his experiences. After two years in the Royal Air Force, Jim Lotz became a trader in West Africa before emigrating to Canada in 1954. Since then he has had a wide range of jobs and served with "Operation Hazen" on Northern Ellesmere Island in 1957-58. He is the author of 16 books, and co-author of two others. The titles include *Canadians at War*, *The Mounties* and *The Sixth of December*, a novel set on the Western Front and during the Halifax Explosion.

The Consulting Editor

Col (Ret'd) John Boileau was born in Moncton, New Brunswick, and entered the Canadian Army in 1962, retiring in 1999. He has served across Canada, in the United States, with the United Nations in Cyprus, twice with NATO forces in Germany and twice in the United Kingdom in various command, training and staff appointments. He is a graduate of the United States Army Armour Officer Advanced Course, the Canadian Forces Command and Staff College and the British Forces Royal College of Defence Studies. He commanded his regiment, Lord Strathcona's Horse (Royal Canadians) from 1985 to 1987 and spent the last five years of his career as the Army Adviser at the Canadian High Commission, London, England.

APPENDIX 1: MILITARY RANKS
(with appreviations used in text)

CANADIAN ARMY	RCAF	RCN
General	Air Marshal	Admiral
Lieutenant General (Lt. Gen)	Air Marshal (A/M)	Vice Admiral (V.Adm.)
Major General (Maj. Gen)	Air Vice Marshal (AVM)	Rear Admiral (R. Adm.)
Brigadier	Air Commodore (A/C)	Commodore (Comm.)
Colonel (Col.)	Group Captain (GC)	Captain (Capt.)
Lieutenant Colonel (Lt.Col)	Wing Commander (W/C)	Commander (Cdr.)
Major	Squadron Leader (S/L)	Lieutenant Commander (Lt. Cdr.)
Captain (Capt.)	Flight Lieutenant (F/L)	Lieutenant (Lt.)
Lieutenant (Lt.)	Flying Officer (F/O)	Sub Lieutenant (Slt.)
Second Lieutenant (2nd Lt.)	Pilot Officer (P/O)	Midshipman
Warrant Officer I (WO I)	Warrant Officer I (WO I)	
Warrant Officer II (WO II)	Warrant Officer II (WO II)	Chief Petty Officer (CPO)
Staff Sergeant (S/Sgt.)	Flight Sergeant (F/Sgt.)	Petty Officer (PO)
Sergeant (Sgt.)	Sergeant (Sgt.)	Leading Seaman
Corporal (Cpl.)	Corporal (Cpl.)	Able Seaman
Lance Corporal (L/Cpl)	Leading Aircraftsman (LAC)	Ordinary Seaman
Private (Pvt.)	Aircraftsman First Class (AC1)	
	Aircraftsman Second Class (AC2)	

Locations where
Canadians participated
in peacekeeping & major humanitarian
aid/disaster relief missions
in the 20th century